COERCIVE DIPLOMACY AGAINST PAKISTAN

Options and Effectiveness in Non-Nuclear Conflict Space in Current Times

COERCIVE DIPLOMACY AGAINST PAKISTAN

Options and Effectiveness in Non-Nuclear Conflict Space in Current Times

Maj Akshat Upadhyay

Centre for Land Warfare Studies
Delhi Cantt
New Delhi

KNOWLEDGE WORLD
KW Publishers Pvt Ltd
New Delhi

First reprint, May 2019

The Centre for Land Warfare Studies (CLAWS), New Delhi, is an independent think tank dealing with contemporary issues of national security and conceptual aspects of land warfare, including conventional and sub-conventional conflicts and terrorism. CLAWS conducts research that is futuristic in outlook and policy-oriented in approach.

Centre for Land Warfare Studies
RPSO Complex, Parade Road, Delhi Cantt, New Delhi 110010
Tel: +91.11.25691308 **Fax:** +91.11.25692347
Email: landwarfare@gmail.com **Website:** www.claws.in
CLAWS Army No. 33098

ISBN 978-93-87324-77-0 Paperback
ISBN 978-93-87324-78-7 ebook

Published in India by
Kalpana Shukla
KW Publishers Pvt Ltd
4676/21, First Floor, Ansari Road, Daryaganj, New Delhi 110002
Tel: +91.11. 43528107 **Email:** production@kwpub.in • kw@kwpub.in
Website: www.kwpub.in

Printed and bound in India

Contents

List of Figures

List of Annexures

Introduction

India and Pakistan achieved unofficial nuclear power status in 1998[1] with nuclear tests conducted by both the neighbouring countries in succession. For India, this was a message to the entire world that it had finally arrived on the international scene with all the attendant glamour and coercive capabilities of an emerging superpower. India, post the nuclear tests concentrated on its economic and social progress while functioning as a stable democracy. The Kargil intrusion, masterminded by the then Pakistani Army Chief, General Pervez Musharraf was an attempt to use the nuclear 'overhang' to coerce India into giving up much-vaunted vantage positions along the entire stretch of National Highway 1A (NH 1A) and target supply convoys to Siachen, another disputed territory in the frozen wastelands beyond NJ 9842 and thereby besiege the forces there and subsequently take control of the heights. What Pakistan did not account for was the sustained political determination of India not to cede an inch of territory to the intruders and the introduction of airpower[2] in an offensive role, something which had not been done since 1971. The Kargil war made the case for limited operations even under the nuclear overhang without the fear of escalation to a nuclear exchange.

In the post-Kargil scenario, after the 2001 Parliament attacks, India ordered Operation Parakram, the massive mobilisation of troops on the Punjab and Rajasthan border. However, the entire nature of international relations had changed due to the events of September 11, 2001. Pakistan had again gained traction in the eyes of the international community, especially the Americans due to the acceptance of its role as a major

1. P. R. Chari, Pervaiz Iqbal Cheema and Stephen P. Cohen, *Four Crises and a Peace Process* (New York, NY: Brookings Institution Press, 2009).
2. Benjamin S. Lambeth, "Airpower at 18,000': The Indian Air Force in the Kargil War," [online] *Carnegie Endowment for International Peace.* https://carnegieendowment.org/2012/09/20/airpower-at-18-000-indian-air-force-in-kargil-war-event-3777, accessed on June 12, 2018.

ally in the War on Terror[3]. India's major lesson from the mobilisation that lasted almost a year was that American pressure could be used against Pakistan to concede something. The idea of compellence, that of using or threatening to use coercive measures to change state policy took root and was effectively applied against the West to tame and control Pakistan[4]. In 2008, the Mumbai attacks happened and India was lost for options to respond[5]. Eschewing military options, it resorted to diplomacy to paint Pakistan as a state sponsor of terrorism on the world forum. With the turn of the decade, it became clear that the attacks on civilians in India had almost ceased and the focus had shifted to attacks on garrisons, almost all in the state of Jammu and Kashmir (J&K). Gurdaspur, Pathankot, Uri and Nagrota all occurred in quick succession and resulted in substantial casualties to the armed forces. This was again part of a new strategy[6] by Pakistan to inject violence into the Kashmir valley and demoralise the armed forces by attacking them continuously. There was also an element of plausible deniability on part of the Pakistani state by helplessly declaring that they themselves were victims of terror and most of the groups attacking the garrisons were not under Pakistani control. The government then initiated a number of steps, most of which could be categorised as compellence measures, with varying degrees of success. However, most of the compellence measures have to function under the overall context of nuclear deterrence and therein lies the major dilemma. For India to effectively motivate Pakistan to stop cross-border terrorism, it needs to display and at worse use coercive measures to force Pakistan to do so, however, India is aware that as soon as the intensity of coercive measures morph, from the diplomatic to the economic to limited and finally full-fledged military options, the risk of forcing Pakistan to react in a manner that is likely to impose unbearable

---

3. Jonathan Beale, "BBC NEWS|World|South Asia|US 'threatened to bomb' Pakistan," [online] *News.bbc.co.uk,* (2018). http://news.bbc.co.uk/2/hi/south_asia/5369198.stm, accessed on June 12, 2018.
4. Ibid.
5. George Perkovich and Toby Dalton, *Not War Not Peace: Motivating Pakistan to Prevent Cross Border Terrorism,* 1st ed. (Oxford University Press, 2016).
6. https://www.livemint.com/, "Understanding Pakistan's New Terror Strategy," [online] (2017). https://www.livemint.com/Opinion/u8qPE1aAPuUG8SXo19SsEO/Understanding-Pakistans-new-terror-strategy.html, accessed on June 12, 2017.

costs on India due to the nuclear overhang, increases. Hence, there is a need to find ways of realising optimum deterrence within the 'No War No Peace' scenario. This monograph is an effort towards analysing the past coercive measures taken by the Indian government, their successes or failures and the efficacy of future measures that can be taken.

Collection of Data

This monograph utilises both primary as well as secondary data sources in the following forms:

- Face-to-face interviews were conducted with retired senior military officers to understand the coercion part in coercive diplomacy. Each interview lasted a minimum of 2 hours per participant and was exhaustive in nature. The participants of the interview were distinguished officers who had held important appointments in the politico-military apparatus of the Indian government. The officers interviewed for this study were: **Maj Gen Pramod Kumar Saighal** (Defence Expert), **Lt Gen Balraj Singh Nagal**, PVSM, AVSM,SM (Former Commander in Chief of Strategic Forces Command and former Director CLAWS), **Lt Gen Philip Campose**, PVSM, AVSM (Former General Officer Commanding in Chief Western Command, former Vice Chief of Army Staff and Distinguished Fellow CLAWS), **Lt Gen Gurmit Singh**, PVSM, UYSM, AVSM,VSM (Former Adjutant General, former 15 Corps Commander and Distinguished Fellow CLAWS) and **Maj Gen Shashi Bhushan Asthana** (Chief Instructor at USI). To get a better understanding of the nuances of diplomacy, **Mr TCA Rangachari, IFS** (Former Ambassador of India to France, Germany and Algeria; Former Director of Academy of International Studies and now Distinguished Fellow Vivekananda International Foundation) was contacted and a lengthy and exhaustive interview was conducted with him.
- A 2-day seminar on the ideology and way of warfighting of Pakistan was conducted by Konark Corps where distinguished speakers such as **Mr G Parthasarthy, Maj Gen GD Bakshi (Retd)** and **Mr Alok Bansal** graced the stage and discussed the impact of jihadi ideology on the Pakistani state, the various operations launched

by the Pakistani Army against terror groups that have targeted the Pakistani state itself and finally the impact of acquisition of nuclear weapons on the Pakistani mindset.

- A questionnaire was designed and sent to a significant audience of national and international journalists, researchers and academics. While some replied to the questions in an exhaustive manner, in some cases, the answers were not as detailed, yet hinted at significant issues. All of them have been incorporated while writing the conclusion of this thesis. Some of the personalities who were contacted and who responded positively were: **Mr Sarral Sharma**, Research Fellow at Institute of Peace and Conflict Studies, **Mr Ramananda Sengupta**, Senior Associate Editor at New Indian Express, **Mr Pinaki Bhattacharya**, Strategic Security Researcher at Observer Research Foundation (ORF), **Ms Dhanasree Jayaram**, Research Scholar at Manipal University and Project Associate at Manipal Advanced Research Group at Department of Geopolitics and International Relations, **Mr Amit Rohan Saksena**, Geopolitical Analyst and Strategic Commentator at Jindal School of International Affairs. Helpful hints and pointers were received from **Dr Harsh V Pant**, Professor of International Relations at King's College London and Distinguished Fellow at Observer Research Foundation.
- Secondary data was collected in the form of Indian English-language newspapers which were referred to for chalking out the chronology of the compellent measures taken by the Indian government.

Respondents Interviewed for the Monograph

A total of 13 people responded with answers, suggestions and pointers. Out of 13, 5 were decorated senior officers from the armed forces with more than three decades of service, each one of them having served either as commander of forces in the Valley, Western border or India's strategic forces. One former diplomat, an ex-Ambassador to France, Algeria and Germany and with experience as a staffer in one of the Indian Consulates in Pakistan and also having served as the Head of Department of International Relations (IR) at a prestigious university, responded with erudite views and reflections of his own. Researchers, both doctoral and postdoctoral, working with various Indian think-tanks responded with suggestions and full-length answers of their own. For a more rounded analysis, a senior editor and head of the foreign affairs department of the New Indian Express was contacted and he obliged with thoughts of his own.

1

Theoretical Construct of Coercive Diplomacy and Various Models of Deterrence and Compellence

To analyse the success or failure of past coercive actions against Pakistan by the Indian government and the likely measures that could be taken in the future, it is important to outline in brief the important facets of coercive diplomacy. Coercive Diplomacy has two components: Deterrence and Compellence.[7] Deterrence theories were designed keeping the Cold War and interstate competition in mind. These theories were adduced in the sanguine knowledge of distance, technology and communication between the two superpowers of the time, that is, the United States and the erstwhile Soviet Union. With the simultaneous emergence of both India and Pakistan as nuclear powers on the international scene and neither of them with the buffer of distance or trust, the nuclear overhang has enthused Pakistan with the idea of utilising proxy actors to bleed India and wrest some initiative from it in Kashmir. The Kargil war in 1999 broke a major myth that limited war could not be waged under the nuclear shadow. Indian restraint to keep the war limited on its own side encouraged Pakistan to step up the frequency and audacity of the attacks. Major attacks were executed in the Indian heartland such as New Delhi[8] and Mumbai[9] by Pakistan-based non-state actors whose aftermaths left Indian policy decision-making in a flux as to what measures

7. Thomas Schelling, *Arms and Influence,* 1st ed. (Yale University Press, 1966).
8. Richa Taneja, "Parliament Attack Anniversary: Here's What Happened On December 13, 2001, And After," [online] *NDTV.com,* (2011). https://www.ndtv.com/india-news/parliament-attack-anniversary-heres-what-happened-on-december-13-2001-and-after-1787198, accessed on October 07, 2017.
9. Angel Rabasa et al., *The Lessons of Mumbai* (Online Research Library: Questia, 2004). [online] https://www.questia.com/library/120080764/the-lessons-of-mumbai, accessed on May 05, 2017.

could be taken to motivate or compel Pakistan to stop cross-border terror attacks and/or demobilise the major jihadi groups inside the country. In the post-Mumbai scenario, the battlefield has shifted to military garrisons, predominantly in the state of J&K. Terrorists are willing to take on the armed forces of the state in pitched gun battles. An unstable deterrence has emerged between the two South Asian neighbours, punctuated by major, minor and intermediate-scale attacks on targets all across India. Majority of the studies concerned with Indo-Pak relations in terms of coercion focus on events pre-Kargil[10] or Operation Parakram[11]. Post Kargil, Indian compellence measures have had to work under an overarching frame of an unstable deterrence, made worse by both sides' declaration of their nuclear power status and with Pakistan's willingness to use this as a buffer to push in proxies into Kashmir. This is a unique scenario and there is, therefore, a need for studying the coercive measures taken by the Indian government against Pakistan in the wake of intermediate-level attacks in the post-Kargil era, especially post-Mumbai attacks. This monograph focuses on the series of coercive diplomacy measures taken by the Indian government post Kargil with the assumption of analysing the unilateral actions of the Indian government in terms of measures taken, desired results, timeline given, and the stage of stoppage of the compellence policy without going into the details of the Pakistani establishment's decision-making process.

Majority of the studies have focused on the crises between the two countries in the past such as Brasstacks (1987), Kashmir crisis (1990), Kargil (1999) or the Twin Peaks Crisis (2001/02). All these studies, though exhaustive on their own, take the entire incidents as a whole but do not concentrate on particular aspects of the various crises. Compellence measures taken as a subset of the unstable deterrence in South Asia between India and Pakistan have never been studied. No major study of deterrence measures has been conducted of incidents that occurred post Parakram, such as the Mumbai attacks of 2008,

---

10. Sumit Ganguly and Devin Hagerty, *Fearful Symmetry: India-Pakistan Crises in the Nuclear Shadow,* 1st ed. (Washington DC: University of Washington Press, 2006).
11. V. K. Sood and Pravin Sawhney, *Operation Parakram* (New Delhi: Sage Publications, 2006).

though a RAND study in the immediate wake of the Mumbai attacks did take place which was not very detailed in its analysis due to the lack of major data. Intermediate-level attacks on garrisons, which have now become more frequent also have not been analysed for the measures taken to punish or motivate Pakistan to stop militant groups from conducting these attacks. Moreover, most of the analysis has been carried specifically for a Western and more particularly American audience and their policy-makers and not for Indian policymakers. This monograph aims to fill that vacuum.

Military garrisons are strategic structures, generally placed to provide a base of support for troops operating in forward areas. These garrisons, in operational areas, provide logistics, communication and administrative support to the troops deployed ahead. They also serve as places for rest and recoup. Most of the garrisons are afforded heavy protection, adequate vantage points and check posts for their security. Generally, these garrisons acquire a permanent character in a particular area due to the protracted nature of operations. Points of ingress and egress and daily routine of the soldiers can be adjudged based on local human intelligence and observation. In counterinsurgency (CI) areas, the security of the garrison is undermined by the almost regular shifting of troops, mobile nature of operations which emphasises offence rather than defence and a fortress-like mentality of the impregnability of the defenders. Garrisons also occupy a place of prestige in the psyche of the armed forces due to the emphasis on garrison security in daily briefings. The attack on garrisons affect the morale and psyche of the armed forces involved in CI operations and consequently of the nation. Three attacks that occurred almost in succession, that is, Gurdaspur, Pathankot and Uri were all attacks on military garrisons that caused significant casualties to the armed forces personnel and also revealed the new nature of the threat from Pakistan. Post 2008, there was significant pressure on Pakistan to rein in the militant factions and there have been no attacks on civilians in India since. However, the new strategy has revealed a renewed offensive by the Islamist militants, egged on and guided by the Pakistani army inside the Kashmir Valley to demonstrate the fallibility of the Indian Army and its ability to protect the civilians, thereby breeding a new Islamist-dominated narrative, aiming to establish *sharia* in the Valley. The Indian media, encouraged by acknowledgement of the government as a force multiplier during the Kargil War, has been increasingly vocal and right wing, dissuading moderate voices to deal with Pakistan, and breeding an environment of jingoism throughout the country. After the Uri attacks, when soldiers were killed, most of them during their sleep and burned alive,[12] the furore across the nation reached feverish heights, impossible to contain. The government responded by a diplomatic onslaught which finally culminated in the controversial 'surgical strikes' on camps across the Line of Control (LoC). As these attacks are intermediate-level attacks and below the threshold level of Mumbai-style attacks, which the government unofficially and privately has set for itself as a benchmark for responding to Pakistan, it is likely that India can face more attacks of this nature rather than threshold-pushing attacks such as Mumbai. The study of the range of options that the Indian government can use to motivate Pakistan to stop these attacks and finally demobilise the terror groups and their sponsors then assumes urgency.

Broad Definition of Coercive Diplomacy

In the current international system, the use of force generally discriminates peace from war. However, international relations and their related politicking take place in a grey region, which may be characterised as no peace and no war wherein the threat of violence—more than its mere application—is the critical variable for an understanding of interstate relations and crises. The threat of use of violence, and not the actual violence itself, to make the adversary give up something valuable to him or prevent him from taking something valuable from us, in layman's term, is known as coercion or coercive diplomacy. The difference from the brute force is that of choice.

In more technical terms, coercion is the use of threats to influence the behaviour of another (usually a target state but at times a non-

---

12. Firstpost, A Year on from Uri Attack: Surgical Strikes, Elimination of Terrorists and Everything Else that Happened after Audacious Raid," [online] *Firstpost,* (2017). https://www.firstpost.com/india/a-year-on-from-uri-attack-surgical-strikes-elimination-of-terrorists-and-everything-else-that-happened-after-audacious-raid-4054609.html, accessed on January 18, 2018.

state actor) by making it choose to comply rather than forcing it to comply (i.e. by brute force).[13] Some authors separate deterrent and compellent threats. As against threats made to cause an opponent not to take an action, that is, deterrent threats, compellent threats are made to cause an opponent to stop a current action or to undertake another.[14] As Schelling explained in *Arms and Influence,* deterrence and compellence are merely two types of coercive threats, the difference being that "the threat that compels rather than deters often requires that the punishment be administered until the other acts, rather than if he acts."[15]

Deterrence, better known of the two due to its massive applicability during the Cold War era, is the threat to use force in retaliation if the opponent takes a certain action. Compellence, on the other hand, is the use of threats to make a target stop an action it has already undertaken, or to take an action that the coercer wants. Compellence is assumed to be more difficult to achieve due to the necessity of continuously administering a punishment which may or may not be within the capabilities of the coercer. Compellence also requires the inevitable display of some of the coercive capabilities that may be hidden when applying deterrence, where the threat of punishment or the bluff of threat may be as effectively used[16]. For deterrence to be successful, target states just have to maintain the status quo, default inaction is considered to be face-saver. In contrast, compellence involves an obvious change in behaviour, acquiescence to the demands of the coercer, that could be costly in terms of prestige and domestic and international legitimacy.[17]

13. Maria Sperandei, "Bridging Deterrence and Compellence: An Alternative Approach to the Study of Coercive Diplommacy," *International Studies Review* [online] vol. 8, no. 2, 2006, pp. 253–280. https://onlinelibrary.wiley.com/doi/abs/10.1111/j.1468-2486.2006.00573.x, accessed on June 05, 2017.
14. Thomas Schelling, *Arms and Influence,* 1st ed. (Yale University Press, 1966).
15. Ibid.
16. Karl Mueller, "Strategies of Coercion: Denial, Punishment, and the Future of Air Power,"*Security Studies*, [online] vol. 7, no. 3, 1998, pp. 182–228. https://www.tandfonline.com/doi/abs/10.1080/09636419808429354, accessed on December 14, 2017.
17. David Carter, "The Compellence Dilemma: International Disputes with Violent Groups," *International Studies Quarterly*, [online] vol. 59, no. 3, 2015, pp.461–476. https://onlinelibrary.wiley.com/doi/abs/10.1111/isqu.12192 accessed on December 30, 2017.

Compellence is also known as coercive diplomacy, military coercion, coercive military strategy and strategic coercion.

Compellence, then, depends on two factors: **Credibility** (whether the target believes that the coercer will execute its threats) and **Persuasiveness** (whether the threats will have a great impact on the target). Credibility normally depends on whether the coercer has a reputation for carrying out threats that it makes. Persuasiveness comes from the ability to exploit the leverages that the coercer is supposed to have over its target/adversary. If the coercer has adequate leverage over the target in terms of economic, trade or diplomatic measures and has displayed behaviour of executing threats in the past, the chances of a successful compellence action are strong.

Use of Force in Coercive Diplomacy

IR scholars are divided into three camps with respect to the use of force in coercive diplomacy: Coercion through Diplomacy separate from the Use of Force, Coercion exercised almost Entirely through the Use of Force and Coercion exercised by both Diplomacy and Force.[18] Their brief description is given below.

Coercion through Diplomacy Separate from the Use of Force

This school of thought believes that if the coercer has had to resort to the actual resort of force then the implication is that coercion has failed. Application of force amounts to a failure of coercive diplomacy. The threat of force is latent and never to be used. This type of latent force also affords the coercer much greater mileage in conducting diplomatic negotiations. However, the difference in power projection capabilities should be wide enough. For this school, coercion is an outcome produced by clear signalling and orchestration.[19]

---

18. Patrick C. Bratton, "When is Coercion Successful?," *Naval War College Review*, [online] vol. 58, no. 3, 2005. http://digital-commons.usnwc.edu/nwc-review/vol58/iss3/6/, accessed on September 13, 2017.
19. Alexander L. George and William Simons, *Limits of Coercive Diplomacy,* 2nd ed. (Michigan: Westview Press, 1994).

Coercion Exercised Almost Entirely through the Use of Force

Coercion is a process that happens during the use of force, or during the actual use of measures such as economic sanctions. Coercion is the use of force to get the target to comply with the demands of the coercer but without completely destroying the military forces of the target state[20]. The major problem for this school, however, is that it is hard to distinguish clearly between coercion and brute force.

Coercion Exercised by Both Diplomacy and Force

There is no sharp distinction between coercion without force and that exercised only through force. Coercion includes both signals sent by diplomatic and military means and the actual use of force. The difference between coercion and brute force, according to this camp, is that force is used in a measured and controlled way to signal to the target the threat of further punishment unless it complies. The increasing use of force, in a measured and connected way, is a means of driving home the coercive threat, not necessarily representing the failure of coercion.

The state or entity attempting coercion must be aware of the centre of gravity, of the target state or entity, either tangible such as population, military or some such or intangible such as will, perception, that "if destroyed, would cause the enemy's resistance to collapse...only by threatening the state's centre of gravity can a coercer compel the greatest concessions from the target state." Coercers must know a great deal about the target regime's composition and internal political struggles in order to shape their policies in a way that maximises the influence of those in the target state's government whose hopes and fears are most compatible with the coercer's objectives. Care must be taken that this faction(s) must also be of a considerable, if not the most, influence within the target state.

Generally, deterrence and compellence have been taken as separate and mutually exclusive events. But the study of cases in past history point towards a linkage, either in parallel or sequential. Most of the studies of coercive diplomacy treat deterrence and compellence as separate halves of a strategy, which may be applied in an either/or

20. Mueller, n. 16.

format. These studies fail to gauge the complexity of each case study being a complex mix of both deterrence and compellence scenarios. As a result, the measures that are formulated to address these situations are not completely successful, due to a misreading of the situation.

Theories of Deterrence and Compellence

The major theories that define the relationship between deterrence and compellence are given below.

Joint But Opposite

Major theorists that ascribe to this school of thought are Thomas Schelling, Paul Lauren, Gordon Craig and Alexander George. This school of thought believes that deterrence is indefinite in timing and tactically static; it involves setting the stage by demanding inaction and, potentially, waiting forever for the opponent to act. The compellent threat, in contrast, cannot wait forever to be effective. A demand has to be formulated, a deadline fixed, and some punitive action, to be ceased if the adversary yields, has to be put in motion[21]. Thus, whereas the issuing of a threat is sufficient for deterrence, both the threat and the exemplary use of force are required for compellence.

Deterrence–Compellence Divide

This school of thought treats deterrence and compellence as two separate theories. The massive increase in destructive firepower brought about by nuclear and thermonuclear weapons soon after the rise of the Iron Curtain marked the Golden Age of deterrence. Theorists defined the characteristics of these two instruments of coercive diplomacy and laid the foundation for the distinction between deterrence and compellence as two separate concepts. This school of thought gives prime importance to deterrence. After the end of the Cold War, with the dawn of unipolarity and ascent of the United States, the utility of compellence was discovered in a number of instances such as Iraq,

21. Paul Gordon Lauren, "Ultimata and Coercive Diplomacy," *International Studies Quarterly*, vol. 16, no. 2, 1972, pp. 131–166. https://doi.org/10.2307/3013977, accessed on November 23, 2017.

Somalia, Bosnia, Libya, Laos, Cuba and Haiti, all by the US military power. Compellence seemed to offer practical and analytical promise, and the unequal treatment of the two branches of coercion began to be redressed.

Blurring of Boundaries

The divide between deterrence and compellence was critiqued by thinkers such as David Baldwin who stated that the differentiation between the two policies of coercion was deficient because "from a purely semantic standpoint any deterrent threat can be stated in compellent terms and any compellent threat can be stated in deterrent terms."[22] Schelling himself has acknowledged the possibility that the boundaries between deterrence and compellence may blur in certain instances. Mr Freedman observed that the United States was simultaneously conveying two warnings to the Soviet Union: one (compellent) aimed at stopping Soviet missile installations in Cuba, the other (deterrent) aimed at stopping any additional missiles from passing through the US blockade.[23] An entire crisis is seen as a continuous interplay between the two policies of coercion and the standard differentiation between deterrence and compellence is sometimes inadequate to explain the dynamic nature of the crisis and its included moves and countermoves.

Distinctive and Linked

A fourth and upcoming school treats deterrence and compellence as sequentially linked. In the management of a crisis, deterrent and compellent measures have to be seen as being applied sequentially, rather than separately or fused with one another. Either the failure of deterrence is followed by a compellent threat or the success of compellence is followed by a deterrent policy. The success of deterrence or the failure of compellence do not have to be studied as the former would not require any following compellent threat, and the latter would result in war rather than deterrence. In this fourth approach, the analysts'

22. David A. Baldwin, "Power Analysis and World Politics: New Trends versus Old Tendencies," *World Politics*, [online] vol. 31, no. 2, 1979, pp. 161–194. http://www.jstor.org/stable/2009941, accessed on October 22, 2017.
23. Lawrence Freedman, *Deterrence* (Polity, 2004).

focus is on the dynamic process leading from the failure of deterrence to the issuing of a final compellent threat.[24]

A New Model of Coercive Diplomacy for the Indian Subcontinent

The above-mentioned theories encapsulate all academic thinking about coercive diplomacy since the Cold War. However, what these theories assumed was the safety of distance that separated the United States and the former Union of Soviet Socialist Republics, the safety from the danger of Mutually Assured Destruction (MAD), the safety of technology that would prevent an accidental launch of nuclear warheads and finally the safety of ideology that no state could afford to be self-destructive in its nature. Unfortunately, the situation in the Indian subcontinent negates all these assumptions: India and Pakistan are neighbours, as close as two neighbours can be; neither of the countries has mega city-busting bombs or massive countervalue targeting capabilities that could trigger MAD; the technological kill-switches that are supposed to safeguard against any accidental launches are questionable at best and finally, Pakistan is on the brink of implosion, with jihadi groups and militias challenging the state's monopoly of violence and, hence, its sovereignty. There is also a grave danger of 'reverse indoctrination' of the Pakistani Army, leading to doubts regarding its capability to handle and protect the nuclear arsenal.

India and Pakistan's quandary has been accentuated by the ideological and existential enmity that Pakistan harbours against its giant neighbour. This has led to the emergence of the Pakistani army at the helm of affairs in the state, cannibalising its own society for its power games. Use of proxies in the 1947/48 war and similarly in the 1965 war and the apparent and the advertised success of the mujahideen in Afghanistan against the Russians encouraged the Pakistani Army to use these proxies against India in Kashmir and *bleed it by a thousand cuts.*[25] Slowly and steadily

24. Eric Herring, *Danger and Opportunity: Explaining International Crisis Outcomes,* 1st ed. (Manchester: Manchester University Press, 1995).
25. Maninder Dabas, "Here are Major Long Term War Doctrines Adopted by India and Pakistan over the Years," *Idiatimes,* https://www.indiatimes.com/news/india/with-tensions-soaring-high-once-again-here-are-major-war-doctrines-exercised-by-india-pakistan-over-the-years-262273.html, accessed on June 12, 2017.

the power of these jihadi groups went on increasing as did the number of their cadres till they were able to challenge the writ of the Pakistani state. Major incidents such as the raid on the Red Mosque in Islamabad[26] coalesced these disparate groups into an entity that threatens the very existence of Pakistan as a state. Army-sponsored proxies, especially in Punjab have attracted followers in the million.[27] While some still obey the orders from the army top brass, some naturally have started carving their own path.[28] A mix of these actors, encouraged and guided by the retired and serving members of the Inter-Services Intelligence, caused the Parliament attacks of 2001 and the Mumbai attacks of 2008. In both these cases, Indian response, massive mobilisation on the Punjab and Rajasthan borders and diplomatic onslaught respectively, failed to elicit any major responses from the Pakistani state, secure in their belief that the nuclear 'overhang' protected them from any major Indian military retaliation.

This, therefore, forms the basis of a new theory of nested compellence that this dissertation will try to substantiate based on primary and secondary data. This theory will be first explained with the help of a figure and subsequently explained in detail.

26. Khaled Ahmed, *Sleepwalking to Surrender* (n.d.).
27. Ibid.
28. Sood and Sawhney, n. 11.

Figure 1.1: Diagrammatic representation of nested compellence

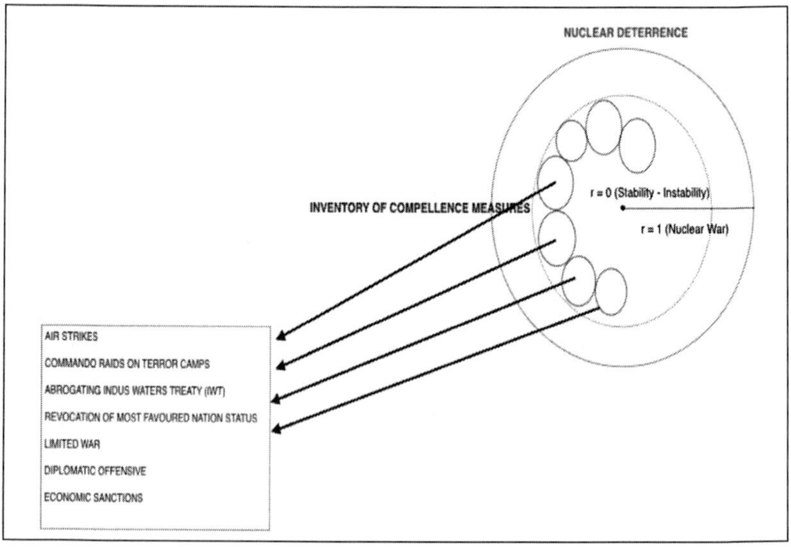

The diagram here denotes a group of circles. The outermost circle indicates the nuclear deterrent that is touching or crossing the circles amounts to a destructive nuclear war, which has to be avoided at all costs. The inner circle, that is, with the dotted lines denotes the compellence circle. This is a dynamic circle whose radius r can vary from zero to one. When the radius r = 0, that means the absence of any situation or condition that warrants use of coercive diplomacy by India. This is also the prevalence of the stability–instability paradox which basically says that the mutual possession of nuclear weapons in an adversarial context gives both parties a strong interest in avoiding resorting to a full-scale war for fear of escalation to the nuclear level. However, the mutual recognition of the danger of large-scale conflict also leads states to undertake probing actions at lower levels of conflict in the expectation that the risks of such probes are both controllable and calculable. The nuclear weapons provide stability on the macro level but instability at the micro level. In fact, this paradox can also be described as a vicious circle; stability at the macro level encourages and leads to instability at micro level which then has to be resolved through diplomatic means or brinkmanship gestures, which invariably leads to instability at macro level, again starting the vicious circle that normally characterises relations between India and Pakistan. If an incident occurs, which is sufficiently warranted by India to initiate compellence measures against Pakistan, depicted by the small circles under the overall inner dotted circle of compellence, the intensity of the compellence measures will dictate the size of the blue circle and overall the size of the compellent threat that India can pose to Pakistan. Slowly and steadily, as the radius of the inner dotted circle increases with the increase in intensity of compellence measures against Pakistan in case of Pakistan not adhering to India's demands, the maximum compellent threat, that is, of limited or a protracted war will invariably push the inner dotted circle to the very near and dangerous proximity of the outer circle of nuclear deterrence. As soon as this circle is touched or crossed, deterrence will fail and nuclear war will ensue.

In the context of the Indian subcontinent, therefore, the inventory of compellent measures has to be applied keeping in mind the nuclear deterrence in mind. This gives Pakistan a lot of leverage in terms of not complying with Indian demands, as it knows that India cannot push Pakistan beyond a certain point, without invoking the nuclear option. Since it is generally aware of the limits of Indian coercion, Indian coercive diplomacy has to function within that very narrow corridor of $0<r<1$ where r can be zero but never one. It is the aim of this dissertation to study this nested compellence relationship by analysing various Indian compellent measures taken by India in the aftermath of attacks on Indian military garrisons in the post-Kargil scenario.

2

Coercion in The Context of Indo-Pakistan Relations (Pre- and Post-Kargil)

Aim of Kargil Intrusion

Before beginning with the analysis of coercive diplomacy or compellent measures taken by India against Pakistan in the wake of attacks on garrisons in the post-Kargil scenario, it is pertinent to point out the differences in approach, if any, pre- and post-Kargil. Here, the Kargil war has been taken as the dividing line as it was the first limited conflict to have taken place between the two nuclear-armed neighbours, almost immediately after the declaration of their nuclear status. This war brought out some stark lessons, both for the Indian as well as the Pakistani sides. For Pakistan, this war was supposed to be its 'moment of glory',[29] the fruition of a long-shelved plan that would take important real estate on the Indian side of the LoC, besiege Indian forces at Siachen and internationalise the Kashmir issue, a major feat indeed. Infiltrating troops of the Northern Light Infantry, a paramilitary at the time, under the charade of well-prepared *mujahideen*, were pushed inside the Indian side of the LoC in the Kargil, Dras, Batalik and Mushkoh sectors.[30] Stocks for a prolonged occupation had already been preplaced and positions were well-built and fortified by the time the intrusion was detected. Pakistan considered itself safe under the nuclear umbrella, betting on the pusillanimity of the Indian politicians and the 'winner takes all' concept at the LoC. The Pakistani army had calculated that by the time negotiations were underway for the cessation of hostilities, they would already have changed the alignment of the LoC in their favour,

29. Christine Fair, *Fighting to the End: The Pakistan Army's Way of War,* 1st ed. (Oxford: Oxford University Press, 2014).
30. Myra MacDonald, *Defeat is an Orphan*, 1st ed. (Penguin Random House India, 2017).

captured dominating heights along NH 1A, forcing India to negotiate on Siachen.[31] What Pakistan could not imagine was India launching a mini war to recapture all the heights, with artillery and the use of air power, not seen since 1971.[32] A lesson was learned that there were strategic windows that could be exploited, even with the nuclear weapons coming into the equation. Kargil, however, was a defensive war and the compellent scenario should not be seen to be applied here. It is only after this war that military and diplomatic strategies to use coercion against Pakistan began to take shape, though in an amorphous form and still not crystallised into a National Security Plan. By the same token, it is important to emphasise that unlike in the 1965 war when India resorted to horizontal escalation within the span of 1 week, in the Kargil conflict, the Indian politico-military leadership carefully confined the ambit of conflict to the areas where the Pakistani forces breached the LoC, also strictly forbidding the Indian forces to not cross the LoC into the Pakistani side, in hot pursuit.

Kargil to Mumbai

India has used compellent measures once before the Kargil scenario, against Pakistan, when the convergence of political willingness and military daredevilry initially enabled India to conduct a massive show of force to Pakistan. Though it was ultimately unsuccessful in fulfilling its aim, the failure itself brought out various lessons to be put to use later. Especially in the pre-Kargil scenario, the reason for using these measures was connected to the Sikh insurgency and not like the case in the aftermath of the explosion of violence in the Kashmir valley after the late 1980s. After the infiltration of Pakistani proxies in the form of Pakistani and other foreign militants, hijacking the indigenous insurgency, Indian demand has been firm and singular. This has been expressed at various regional and international forums on numerous occasions. India wants the total cessation of cross-border terrorism from Pakistan and for Pakistan to demobilise the major groups and organisations involved in the same. Even after Kargil, India was subjected

31. V. P. Malik, *Kargil: From Surprise To Victory,* 2nd ed. (Harper Collins, 2011).
32. Lambeth, n. 2.

to a horrifying number of terrorist incidents, leading to a huge loss of lives. India's attempts at linking Pakistan to terrorism almost fell on deaf ears in the international community. It was only after the September 11 attacks on the United States homeland that the international community finally took cognisance of the terror emanating from Pakistan and its neighbouring Afghanistan. However, due to the vicissitudes of the international climate, it was India's turn to be jolted after Pakistan, however reluctant and resistant, became the hub of America's Global War on Terror (GWOT). Operation Parakram, the mass mobilisation of close to half a million men on the borders of Punjab and Rajasthan, meant to coerce Pakistan to agree to India's demands, was resorted to, after the brazen attack on the Indian Parliament on December 13, 2001.[33] Mumbai's commuter train system and Mumbai's heartland were bombed and attacked respectively in 2005 and 2008.

Operation Brasstacks: Initial Conditions

Launched in November 1986, Brasstacks was a year-long Indian military exercise that sparked a three-month crisis. India's first female Prime Minister had been assassinated on October 30, 1984, by her two Sikh bodyguards, who considered the desecration of their holiest shrine, the Golden Temple, by the Indian army a sacrilege.[34] Her pilot son, with no interest in political affairs, was appointed as the Prime Minister. Though there was an attempt by the new leadership to expand upon the policies of economic reforms that had been initiated by Mrs Gandhi in her last days, the foreign and security policy imperatives remained the same: India was to follow the dictates of non-alignment, emphasise upon North–South dialogue and maintain the robust arms transfer mechanism with the Soviet Union.[35]

Military Modernisation and the Emergence of Gen Sundarji

One thing that distinguished this administration from the previous ones was the emphasis on military modernisation. This was due to several

33. Sood and Sawhney, n. 11.
34. Mark Tully and Satish Jacob, *Amritsar: Mrs Gandhi's Last Battle,* 2nd ed. (New Delhi: Rupa Publications, 2010).
35. Chari, Cheema and Cohen, n. 1.

reasons. For 2.5 years, the Indian and Pakistani armies had been firing at each other regularly on the Siachen Glacier.[36] Each side suspected the other of trying to grab control of the glacier and its environs and of supporting separatist movements across the border: Pakistan was alleged to be supporting the Sikhs and Kashmiris in India, and India the Sindhis in Pakistan, reviving memories there of the secession of East Pakistan from Pakistan in 1971. The atmosphere was already clouded by several earlier war scares over possible attacks on Pakistan's nuclear facilities. To add to the strain, the Soviet occupation of Afghanistan had produced a massive influx of refugees into Pakistan and transformed Pakistan into a Frontline State, in Cold War parlance. The military regime of Gen Zia-ul-Haq had been courted by the United States in order to prosecute a covert war against the Soviets in Afghanistan. The Reagan administration had, as early as 1981, granted Pakistan a 5-year arms and economic assistance package totalling $3.2 billion.[37] Included in this package was the much coveted F-16 aircraft which would give the Pakistani Air Force (PAF) a qualitative edge over India's Soviet-supplied MiGs.[38] In 1986, as this package came to a close, the United States renewed its assistance to Pakistan over India's objections and granted it another $4.02 billion over the next 6 years. Given Pakistan's significant military modernisation, a realisation dawned among the Indian security community dominated by think-tanks, academics and retired and serving military and intelligence services officers that there was an increased threat from Pakistan. Apart from this structural change, the Soviet Union not wanting a disgruntled India over the occupation of Pakistan provided India with substantial amounts of military hardware. Also, PM Rajeev Gandhi and Arun Singh, his Minister of State for Defence and his close friend, were military enthusiasts. They found an ideal counterpart in their quest for military modernisation, in Gen Krishnaswamy Sundarji, the Indian Army Chief of Army Staff, who was interested in providing greater mobility and manoeuvrability into India's armoured formations and introduced the concept of mechanised infantry into the Indian Army. Sundarji was also a proponent of the use of

36. Sood and Sawhney, n. 11.
37. Husain Haqqani, *Magnificent Delusions,* 3rd ed. ([Place of publication not identified]: Perseus Books Group, 2013).
38 Chari, Cheema and Cohen, n. 1.

'dissuasion' which required the clear communication of a threat, making the threat credible and possessing the requisite military capabilities to carry out the threat. Sundarji had been inspired by the Western theories of nuclear deterrence and was the first one to ponder over the question of the interaction of conventional and nuclear forces in battlefield conditions in the subcontinent.[39]

Hijacking of IC-814

Between Kargil and the start of a concerted campaign to attack Indian military garrisons with effect from 2013, India faced four major and a host of minor terrorist incidents involving a huge loss of lives. The incidents and the actions taken by the Indian government in their aftermath are described here in brief. On December 24, 1999, Indian Airlines Flight IC-814 was hijacked by four hijackers from Kathmandu to New Delhi. It was forced to land in Kandahar, in what was then Taliban-infested territory. As per reports and accounts of senior intelligence officers such as Mr Ajit Doval, then head of the Intelligence Bureau (IB) and now the National Security Advisor, the hijackers were briefed and supported by the ISI. Pakistan's involvement was as clear as day, but no one in the international community was able or willing to assist India in solving this problem. After tense days of negotiations, India had no option but to acquiesce to the major demands of the hijackers, that is, the release of three militants, chief among them was Maulana Masood Azhar, now the head of Jaish-e-Mohammad (JeM). After this horrific episode, India had no doubts that the international community was failing to pay enough attention to the threat of international terrorism emanating from Pakistan. India particularly blamed the United States and the United Kingdom for being blinded in their nonrecognition of Pakistan's role as the hub of terrorism.

Operation Parakram

On December 13, 2001, as the Indian parliament was in session, shots rang out in the Parliament House complex. The standoff that ensued between the Indian security forces and those who had attacked the complex

39. P.R. Chari, Pervaiz Iqbal Cheema and Stephen P. Cohen, *Four Crises and a Peace Process* (New York, NY: Brookings Institution Press, 2009).

involved multiple explosions and exchange of hundreds of rounds of fire, which left 12 dead. Once the Government of India concluded that Pakistan-based terrorist groups were responsible and Pakistan refused to take action against them (Islamabad claimed that the allegations lacked evidence), it ordered a full-scale mobilisation of its armed forces and deployed them along the entire India–Pakistan border. Pakistan was asked to cease cross-border terrorism immediately and to hand over some 20 criminals wanted in India, to whom, the Indian government alleged, refuge had been provided in Pakistan. India snapped communications between the two countries, as well as bus and train services and flights of Pakistani aircraft over the Indian territory.[40] It also withdrew its High Commissioner from Islamabad. Pakistan initiated a counter-deployment, and there was a palpable sense that war was imminent. This was especially the case on two occasions after the attack on the Indian parliament: in early January 2002 and in mid-May 2002. On both occasions, the United States intervened to defuse the situation. At Washington's urging, Pakistani president Pervez Musharraf issued statements on both occasions pledging to stop cross-border infiltration into India and disband the jihadi organisations that were sponsoring this activity. This was the riskiest compellent measure that India had ever undertaken and its targets were both Pakistan and the United States. India had stressed that the aim of Operation Parakram was 'to put Pakistan on notice and to signal how seriously the country viewed the attack on its Parliament' and 'to tell the world that India's patience was running out.' Its intention had clearly been to compel Pakistan to end what India perceived as its policy of promoting terrorism in Kashmir, return to India the 20 individuals wanted for criminal or terrorist activity, and to initiate hostilities if that did not happen. Moreover, by threatening war, India had compelled the United States to pressure Pakistan, its new ally in the war on terrorism. In this crisis, India, as opposed to Pakistan, was the one subtly using the threat of a subcontinental war to mobilise the international community against Pakistan. Pakistan's response to the Indian build-up and threatening statements was to mount large-scale counter-deployment of its forces in a manner reminiscent of the Brasstacks exercise of 1987. Pakistan analysts said India's manoeuvres

40. Sood and Sawhney, n. 11.

smacked of 'coercive diplomacy', a strategy of threatening to use force and simultaneously practising diplomacy to achieve a particular objective. Pakistan then pressured the United States into not coming down too heavily on it, in view of Pakistan's deployments on its eastern borders as per GWOT and the need to redeploy that precious manpower on its eastern border with India.

Mumbai Commuter Train Blasts

Seven near-synchronised bomb blasts tore apart the Mumbai local commuter train system on July 11, 2006. The bombs were set off in pressure cookers on trains plying the Western line of the Suburban Railway network. 209 people were killed and over 700 were injured. Investigations pointed to the role of the Indian Mujahideen and the ISI,[41] but since no concrete evidence could link these agencies or their role, no visible action was taken by the Indian government against Pakistan.

Mumbai Attacks (26/11) 2008

The 2008 Mumbai attacks (also referred to as 26/11) were a group of terrorist attacks that took place in November 2008, when 10 members of Lashkar-e-Taiba (LeT), an Islamic terrorist organisation based in Pakistan, carried out a series of 12 coordinated shooting and bombing attacks lasting 4 days across Mumbai. The attacks, which drew widespread global condemnation, began on November 26 and lasted until November 29, 2008, killing 164 people and wounding at least 308. By the early morning of November 28, all sites except for the Taj Hotel had been secured by Mumbai Police Department and security forces.[42] On November 29, India's National Security Guards conducted operations to flush out the remaining attackers. It culminated in the death of the last remaining attackers at the Taj Hotel and ended the attacks. During the course of the attack, one of the attackers, Ajmal Kasab, a Pakistani Punjabi militant was nabbed by the police. During his interrogation,

41. The Hindu. "All You Need to know about the 7/11 Mumbai Train Blasts," [online] *The Hindu,* (2018). http://www.thehindu.com/news/cities/mumbai/all-you-need-to-know-about-711/article7640887.ece, accessed on October 25, 2017.
42. Adrian Levy and Cathy Scott-Clark, *The Siege: The Attack on the Taj,* 1st ed. (Penguin Books Limited, 2015).

he disclosed that the attackers were members of LeT among others. The Government of India said that the attackers came from Pakistan, and their controllers were in Pakistan. On January 07, 2009, Pakistan confirmed the sole surviving perpetrator of the attacks was a Pakistani citizen. At least 164 victims (civilians and security personnel) and 9 attackers were killed in the attacks. Among the dead were 28 foreign nationals from 10 countries. One attacker was captured. The bodies of many of the dead hostages showed signs of torture or disfigurement.[43]

Options Available with India

As per the accounts of Pranab Dhal Samanta, in his article in the Indian Express, when the top Indian national security officials met to discuss the response to these attacks (Samanta, 2010), they realised they did not have any realistic compellent actions to take against Pakistan. A massive mobilisation of the forces, akin to Op Parakram was out of the question. Air strikes against terror camps were suggested but due to lack of real-time intelligence, they were ruled out. In the subsequent meetings, the Army was willing to take a limited ground offensive against Pakistan but warned that it could quickly escalate. There was also the risk of Pakistan misperceiving an Indian conventional strike as a nuclear one and responding in kind. Covert operations against targets in Pakistan-occupied Kashmir (PoK) or Pakistani hinterland were discussed but Research and Analysis Wing admitted to having no assets in Pakistan that could conduct such operations. Commando raids were also discarded as having a limited compellent value and a high probability of a Public Relations nightmare, in case of capture of any of the operatives by the Pakistanis. The PM, therefore, decided not to go ahead with any military options pursuing a course of non-violent pressure and urging others in the international community to join it in condemning Pakistan.[44] However, even these pressures failed to elicit a strong reaction from the United Nations which failed to

43. Ibid.
44. Pranab Dhal Samanta, "11/26/2008: How India Debated a War With Pakistan that November," [online] *Pakistanis for Peace,* (2010). http://archive.indianexpress.com/news/2611-how-india-debated-a-war-with-pakistan-that-november/716240/, accessed on December 20, 2017.

issue a Chapter VII resolution, as it had done in the wake of 9/11 and the 2005 London subway bombings. Economic sanctions were not imposed on Pakistan. The only silver lining was that Pakistan was further isolated and found itself under intense international pressure to prevent similar attacks.[45]

Attacks on Indian Garrisons

A new trend has emerged, especially after the international condemnation of Pakistan in the wake of the 2008 Mumbai attacks, of targeting Indian forces, especially garrisons, the majority of them in the state of J&K. Apart from major attacks such as Uri, Pathankot and Nagrota, following are the array of attacks carried out by terrorists against the Indian armed forces and affiliated forces in the last few years (at the time the data was compiled):

- *March 29, 2017:* Militants opened fire at a police station in south Kashmir's Kulgam district. Nobody was hurt in the attack.
- *November 29, 2016:* Terrorists entered cantonment premises in Jammu city, killing seven soldiers including two officers.
- *November 24, 2016:* Militants attacked Kralgund police station in Handwara tehsil of Kupwara.
- *October 06, 2016:* Attempt to storm a Rashtriya Rifles (RR) camp was foiled when security men gunned down three militants after an exchange of fire in North Kashmir.
- *October 02, 2016:* Heavily armed terrorists attacked a Rashtriya Rifles (RR) army camp where at least two terrorists were killed.
- *September 18, 2016:* Seventeen soldiers were killed in a militant attack in Uri area of Baramulla district. Four militants were killed in the encounter.
- *June 25, 2016:* Eight Central Reserve Police Force (CRPF) personnel were killed and 20 others injured when militants attacked their convoy in Srinagar on Srinagar–Jammu National Highway.
- *February 21, 2016:* Three army commandos, including two Captains and a militant, were killed in a fierce gunfight with a group of terrorists holed up inside a government building on the outskirts of Srinagar.

45. Perkovich and Dalton, n. 5.

- *December 07, 2015:* Six CRPF personnel injured when militants opened fire on their convoy in Bijbehara in South Kashmir's Anantnag District.
- *November 25, 2015:* Three JeM militants and a generator operator of Military Engineering Service were killed when a group of militants attacked an Army camp near Line of Control (LoC) in North Kashmir.
- *November 18, 2015:* A Colonel with the Army's elite Para Commando unit was killed in an encounter with militants in the forests of Kupwara.
- *August 05, 2015:* Militants attacked a convoy of the border guarding force on the Jammu–Srinagar National Highway in Udhampur district.
- *May 31, 2015:* Army foils attack on its Brigade headquarters in Tanghdar sector of Kupwara District by killing four members of six heavily armed militants.
- *March 21, 2015:* A fedayeen attack was carried out at the Army camp on Jammu–Pathankot National Highway. Three persons including one civilian, a Major and an Army jawan were also injured during the attack.
- *March 20, 2015:* A fedayeen squad of militants in Army fatigues stormed a Police Station in Kathua District killing seven persons, including three Special Forces personnel, two civilian and two militants while twelve persons, including eight CRPF personnel, three Policemen and a civilian were also injured in the incident.
- *December 05, 2014:* A group of heavily armed militants stormed into an army camp in Uri Sector of Baramulla District near the LoC. One Lieutenant Colonel and seven soldiers of the Army, one Assistant sub-inspector and two constables of J&K Police were killed. Six militants were also killed in the operation.
- *November 27, 2014:* Ten persons, including four civilians, three Army soldiers and three militants were killed in a day-long encounter at the border village of Kathaar in Arnia sector, close to the International Border, of Jammu District.
- *June 24, 2013:* Attack on a military convoy at Hyderpora, Srinagar.
- *March 31, 2013:* Attack on CRPF camp in Srinagar kills five.

Change of Pakistani Strategy

A clear shift can be discerned in the strategy of terrorist handlers in the Pakistani army and the ISI. Even though 2016 has seen a high number of terrorist attacks, most of them have been aimed at Indian security forces. An attack of 26/11 proportions on civilians is likely to evoke a strong response from the international community. It is worth recalling that a number of foreign nationals were also killed in 26/11. Most of the attacks in the last couple of years have also happened in J&K—the Gurdaspur attack (2015) was a notable exception. So, Rawalpindi's strategy is very clear: attack the 'occupying forces' of India in J&K.[46] To support this strategy, the Pakistan Army has, in parallel, supported the protests against the Indian state in the Kashmir valley and elevated the rhetoric on Kashmir on global forums. The ceasefire violations have also increased to help push a greater number of infiltrators inside Kashmir to take advantage of the disaffection in the state. This argument is important because terrorist groups that are not supported by a state will not have an incentive to make the shift in strategy that the Pakistan-based groups have made. Over the years, the patience in India—and the world—for suffering terrorist attacks is wearing thin. It is for this reason that the United States intervened immediately after both Kaluchak and also 26/11 but not after Uri. India made full use of the latitude available to launch the surgical strikes. While the domestic protests in Kashmir have hurt India, Pakistan's attempt to internationalise 'occupation' of Kashmir has not succeeded. On the contrary, India has gone about raising the problems in Balochistan, including in the United Nations General Assembly (UNGA). Also, a point which has to be clearly pointed out is the increasing level of ambiguous command and control and the hastening ad-hocism in the ISI with respect to the armed cadres of the different groups operating in Kashmir. ISI has had to fight hard to keep the control of the groups from slipping away and enable them to be autonomous groups. The Mumbai and Uri attacks may be a part of the failing system. As is clear from the above incidents of attacks on garrisons, almost all of them in J&K, Pakistan has deliberately kept the level of attacks small scale, and only in certain cases have the attacks

46. https://www.livemint.com, n. 6.

been intermediate. The narrative of an indigenous freedom struggle among the Kashmiris, already exemplified by the stone throwing and vitriol on streets has been established. The attack on 'occupying forces' in the state is a logical conclusion to these protests. The level of violence has been calibrated to not evoke any international condemnation, nor is it deemed hurtful enough to cause a serious reaction from India. Uri was also meant to be a similar kind of action, an attack on a Brigade headquarters near the LoC which was meant to internationalise the Kashmir issue but keep the casualty level similar to a low level attack or at worst an intermediate-level attack. However, due to the prevailing strong nationalist sentiment in India and the proliferation of pro right-wing news outlets especially in the social media and television, in addition to the staggering number of deaths, Uri suddenly started cresting and dominating the news waves in India. International condemnation and support for India started pouring in from all sides.

3

Analysis of Primary Data

Primary Data

Primary data for this dissertation was taken in the following forms:

- Face-to-face interviews were conducted of retired senior military officers to understand the coercion part in coercive diplomacy. Each interview lasted a minimum of two hours per participant and was exhaustive in nature. The participants of the interview were distinguished officers who had held important appointments in the politico-military apparatus of the Indian government. The officers interviewed for this study were: **Maj Gen Pramod Kumar Saighal** (Defence Expert), **Lt Gen Balraj Singh Nagal**, PVSM, AVSM, SM (Former Commander in Chief of Strategic Forces Command and now Director CLAWS), **Lt Gen Philip Campose**, PVSM, AVSM (Former General Officer Commanding in Chief Western Command, former Vice Chief of Army Staff and now Distinguished Fellow CLAWS), **Lt Gen Gurmit Singh**, PVSM, UYSM, AVSM,VSM (Former Adjutant General, former 15 Corps Commander and now Distinguished Fellow CLAWS) and **Maj Gen Shashi Bhushan Asthana** (Chief Instructor at USI). To get a better understanding of the nuances of diplomacy **Mr TCA Rangachari, IFS** (Former Ambassador of India to France, Germany and Algeria; Former Director of Academy of International Studies and now Distinguished Fellow Vivekananda International Foundation) was contacted and a lengthy and exhaustive interview was contacted with him.
- A 2-day seminar on the ideology and way of warfighting of Pakistan was conducted by Konark Corps, where distinguished speakers such as **Mr G Parthasarthy, Maj Gen GD Bakshi (Retd)** and **Mr Alok Bansal** graced the stage and discussed the impact of jihadi ideology on the Pakistani state, the various operations launched

by the Pakistani Army against terror groups that have targeted the Pakistani state itself and finally the impact of acquisition of nuclear weapons on the Pakistani mindset. Another one-day seminar was held at Konark Corps, presided by former Director General of Military Operations and former Director General Aviation **Lt Gen PR Kumar (Retd)** which focused on the concept of limited war against Pakistan. Inputs from these seminars have also informed the conclusion and recommendations of this thesis.

- A number of questions were asked to a significant audience of national and international journalists, researchers and academics. While some replied to the questions in an exhaustive manner, in some cases, the answers were not as detailed yet hinted at significant issues. All of them have been incorporated while writing the conclusion of this thesis. Some of the personalities who were contacted and who responded positively were: **Mr Sarral Sharma**, Research Fellow at Institute of Peace and Conflict Studies, **Mr Ramananda Sengupta**, Senior Associate Editor at New Indian Express, **Mr Pinaki Bhattacharya**, Strategic Security Researcher at ORF, **Ms Dhanasree Jayaram**, Research Scholar at Manipal University and Project Associate at Manipal Advanced Research Group at Department of Geopolitics and International Relations, Helpful hints and pointers were received from **Dr Harsh V Pant**, Distinguished Fellow at ORF.
- Indian newspapers were referred to for chalking out the chronology of the compellent measures taken by the Indian government.

Respondents Interviewed for the Dissertation

A total of 13 people responded with answers, suggestions and pointers. Out of 13, 5 were decorated senior officers from the armed forces with more than three decades of service, each one of them having served either as commander of forces in the Valley, Western border or India's strategic forces. One former diplomat, an ex-Ambassador to France, Algeria and Germany and with experience as a staffer in one of the Indian Consulates in Pakistan and also having served as the head of the department of IR at a prestigious university, responded with erudite views and reflections of his own. Researchers, both doctoral and post-doctoral, working with various Indian institutions responded with suggestions and full-length answers of their own. For a more rounded analysis, a senior editor and head of the foreign affairs department of the New Indian Express was contacted and he obliged with thoughts of his own.

Design of the Questionnaire

The questionnaire has been designed keeping in mind the complexity of the subject. It is a subjective one and not an objective. Following questions have been asked to the respondents:

- Do you think there is a need for a rulebook, maybe in terms of a defined National Security Policy to deal with such kind of events, where out of a host of options available to the Government, a number of permutations and combinations may be worked out to chalk out an adequate response to coerce Pakistan?
- Post the Uri attacks, there was a lot of talk and rhetoric, especially in the media about 'isolating' Pakistan. Do you think, in today's scenario, that a state can isolate another state? What is the meaning of isolation in the international context?
- Do you think that Track II diplomacy works? Should it be used in conjunction with coercion or as a stand-alone part?
- Do you think that measures such as surgical strikes, threatening to revoke the Most Favoured Nation (MFN) status or the Indus Water Treaty (IWT) have had any compellent effect against Pakistan, to stop its cross-border infiltration and terrorism against India? Is there a need to look at incipient steps in a process or does the end state only matter?
- What, according to you, are the coercive measures or steps that need to be taken in order to pressurise Pakistan to accede to our demand of stopping cross-border infiltration?
- I have chosen this time window as all the conflicts/crises that occurred between the two countries after Kargil were marked by a realisation that limited war could take place under a nuclear umbrella and there was only a limited scope of nuclear blackmail by Pakistan. However, the incidents that I have chosen for my research, that is,

Pathankot and Uri are cases of attacks on military garrisons. More than their tactical or strategic value, they also carry a huge symbolic value. All these attacks solicited a response from the governments at the time and were hugely varied in nature. This showed a non-procedural way of functioning of the government which had its pros and cons. Coming to my thesis, I plan to research on the effectiveness of coercive diplomacy measures that were initiated against Pakistan using these incidents as case studies. I was wondering if you could tell me what impact do the following have

   - Surgical strikes
   - UN Ivy League of Terror speech
   - Forward deployments in Punjab, Rajasthan and Jammu and Kashmir
   - Evacuation of border villages
   - Review of MFN status
   - Review of IWD
- In the aftermath of the Uri attacks, Mr Vikas Swarup, Spokesperson for the Ministry of External Affairs (MEA) in his speech said that blood and water cannot flow together. What do you think are the implications of the speech?
- Can we have an India-specific or South Asian-specific IR where the issues of deterrence and compellence are much more nuanced than existential deterrence and mutually assured destruction?

Requirement of a Rulebook for Reacting to Pakistan

Almost all the military respondents believe that there should be policy guidelines in the form of a National Security Policy but they should be broad and vague. Only reference points should guide the government and the government should have full latitude and flexibility in dealing with Pakistan the way it wants. There is a consensus that set piece or preconceived solutions to any crisis may fail or misfire. One respondent felt that even if there were some steps that the government had kept in its mind to deal with attacks depending on the intensity, they should not be in the public domain, nor should the government be held accountable based on those steps. The same respondent felt that options such as air strikes, limited military offensive or commando raids should be pre-planned but there is no requirement of disclosing them in the public domain at least before they are executed. One respondent felt that all domains including social media, diplomacy and electronics should be used in a synergised form to exercise credible coercive diplomacy, and that there is a need to have some kind of a rulebook of principles and accepted norms. On the other hand, in the academic field, most of the respondents felt that India should have a playbook of sorts and that this should be communicated publicly to the Pakistanis. One of the respondents felt that this communication should be accompanied with private assurances related to continuation of good behaviour. Of the respondents interviewed, within the military, 80 percent believed that there should be no rulebook while only 20 percent felt that there should be a rulebook. Within the academic field, the trend was reversed, with 80 percent affirming the need for a rulebook of sorts with Indian government while only 20 percent were of the opinion that there was no requirement of a rulebook. Care should be taken that the respondents who felt that there should be no rulebook did not believe in the government responding to ad hoc behaviour when dealing with Pakistan in the wake of attacks on military garrisons but felt that there should be guiding principles and not concrete steps which must inform decision-making. The lone diplomat interviewed felt that there was a requirement of a rulebook while the newspaper editor emphasised on the need for broad principles rather than rulebooks. Overall, approximately 59 percent of the respondents said that some kind of rulebook was required while 41 percent disagreed with the proposition.

Figure 3.1: Does India Require a Rulebook when dealing with Pakistan?

Description	Military	Academia	Journalist	Foreign Services
Rulebook Required	1	8	0	1
Rulebook Not Required	4	2	1	0

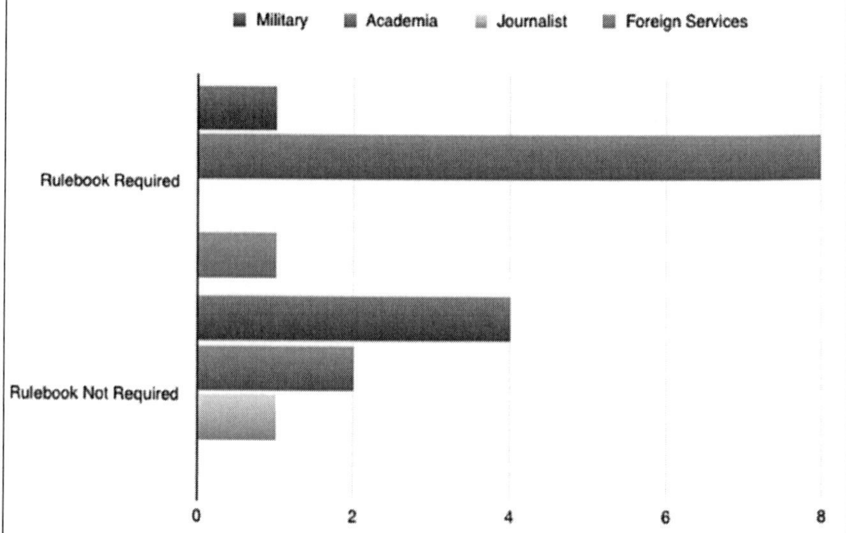

Isolation of Pakistan

This question polarised the subject audience. Within the military, 40 percent believed that isolation of Pakistan was possible and in fact had been achieved by the current government, especially post Uri. Sixty percent were of the opinion that isolation of Pakistan, at least by India was not possible. The reasons given were Pakistan's continuing utility to both the Americans and the Chinese and the hold that these two countries had over the United Nations and other international fora. Those affirming in the positive gave examples of heightened cooperation of the United Arab Emirates and Saudi Arabia and joint statements on terror emanating from Pakistan as examples of India's successful diplomatic efforts to get prime members of Organisation of Islamic Countries (OIC) to side with India. Those opposing the view believed that due to our overemphasis on negating Pakistan, we tended to divulge our sources publicly, inadvertently enabling Pakistan to plug gaps in their security architecture. Also, nonattendance in a South Asian Association for Regional Cooperation (SAARC) summit was not believed by some to be a credible step in isolating Pakistan as it was a dysfunctional body, to begin with. As an example of the West's duplicitous standards, one respondent quoted the thousands of Armoured Personnel Carriers given to Pakistan as Excess Defence Articles[47] and which would then be used by the Pakistanis against Indian forces in an event of war. Respondents pointed out that the United States was heavily dependent on Pakistan's Karachi port and its overland route into Afghanistan for supplying its forces in that theatre. Within the academia, only 20 percent believed that India could successfully isolate Pakistan in the international community. An equal proportion, that is, 40 percent each believed either that Pakistan could not be isolated, or if some directional isolation was also possible, it could either be accomplished through the support of other countries, or be counterproductive. Overall, 23 percent respondents believed that Pakistan could be isolated by India, 53 percent believed that India could never isolate Pakistan and 24 percent believed that some kind of isolation of Pakistan was possible but not by India.

---

47. dawn.com, "Pakistan to get Leftover Afghan War Equipment: Defence Secretary," [online] *Dawn,* (2014). https://www.dawn.com/news/1096837, accessed on November 19, 2017.

Figure 3.2: Is Isolation of Pakistan Possible?

Description	Military	Academia	Journalist	Foreign Services
Isolation Possible	2	2	0	0
Isolation Not Possible	3	4	1	1
Isolation Possible with Caveats	0	4	0	0

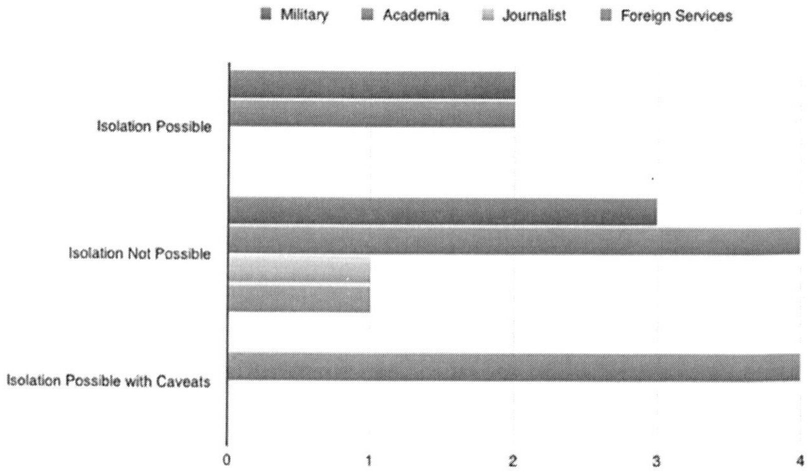

Effectiveness of Track II Diplomacy

This question received a resounding yes from all the respondents. Some caveats, however, were observed. Some believed that Track II diplomacy was always in place and gave the examples of Siachen, Sir Creek and Musharraf's Four Point formula on Kashmir as examples. Some believed that Track II diplomacy required subject experts and dedicated professionals for it to bear fruit and not people who believed in 'photo ops'. There was also an opinion that Track II diplomacy negotiations must be subject-specific and have some kind of a ceiling, in terms of scope and charter.

Figure 3.3: Effectiveness of Track II Diplomacy

Description	Military	Academia	Journalist	Foreign Services
Effective	5	10	1	1
Not Effective	0	0	0	0
Not Certain	0	0	0	0

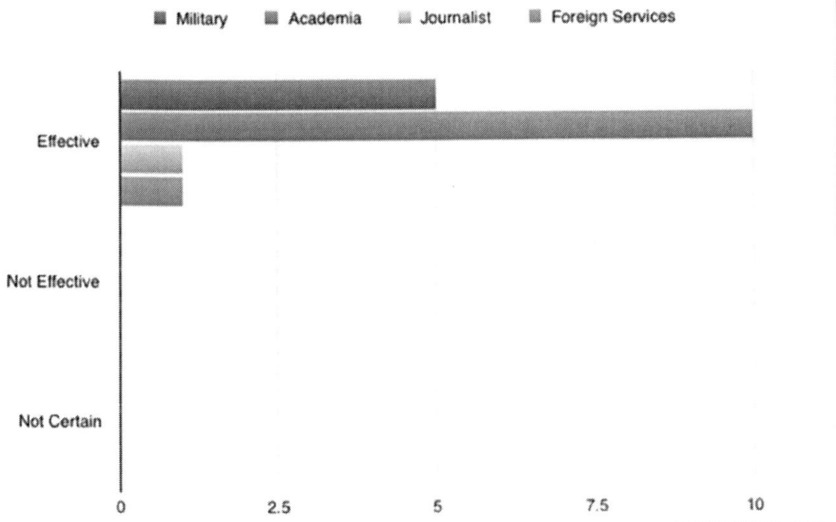

Effectiveness of Compellence Measures

Surgical Strikes

Though everyone felt that the commando raids across the LoC, termed 'Surgical Strikes' by the Indian media and the government were justified, not many were convinced of its coercive value. Many in the military domain lauded the government's efforts to 'do something' that made Pakistan and the world sit up and take notice of the fact that India's sovereignty and the security of its armed forces will not be taken lightly. Not many, however, were convinced of the compellent nature of the action. In fact, when the respondents in the academic field were questioned on the efficacy of the strikes as part of India's coercive strategy, a majority believed that, as a stand-alone gesture or a vindictive measure it was fair game but when it came to coercing Pakistan to dismantle its terror camps, it did not prove that effective. One of the respondents linked the repetitive nature of the terror attacks in India to a growing negative psyche within the Indian citizenry of the inability of India's armed forces to respond in a similar currency. He also bemoaned the absence of a balanced strategic culture in India that either over or underemphasised the role of national security in the state's entire calculus. The biggest advantage of this action, according to the same respondent was the US's deliberate nonaction or noninterference in Indo-Pakistan affairs affording India to take actions of these kinds without any serious international repercussions, a matter of robust Indian foreign policy. Many in the academic field believe that the nature and style of these raids or strikes must be carefully calibrated in order to keep them below a certain threshold pattern that does not give the Pakistani establishment a reason to retaliate, plunging the region into cycles of escalation. Another important fact is that the coercive nature of this act has been mitigated to a large extent by the Pakistani army through its stranglehold over the domestic media, defeating the process of coercion to a large extent. This needs to be looked at. Overall, 24 percent of the respondents felt that the surgical strikes were effective as a coercive measure, while close to 30 percent felt that they were not effective as part of a compellence strategy. A large majority, that is 47 percent, felt that they were not certain of its effectiveness as part of compellence.

Figure 3.4: Surgical Strikes

Description	Military	Academia	Journalist	Foreign Services
Effective	2	2	0	0
Not Effective	0	5	0	0
Not Certain	3	3	1	1

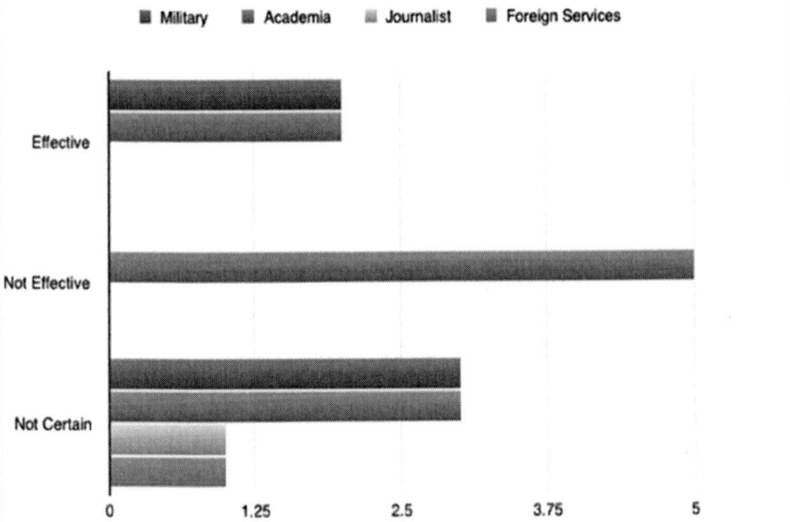

Withdrawal from the Indus Waters Treaty (IWT)

With regards to the IWT, most of the members feel that this is the most effective compellent measure that India has in its armoury. However, this is also the most difficult to achieve, since successful coercion also requires a display of capability and intent. Also, most respondents feel that since India wants to be seen as a responsible and mature international power, it will not revoke this treaty, underwritten by the World Bank, and shunned internationally. Also, Pakistan has played the human rights card in a forceful manner and shifted the blame on its future troubles on the upper riparian. Also, many believe that China could enter the fray in favour of Pakistan and behave in the same manner with India, stopping the flow of Indus at its source in Tibet. A lot of respondents feel that even if India utilises fully the 20 percent of water authorised under the treaty, it will be able to squeeze Pakistan immensely. Overall, 24 percent of the respondents felt that IWT was effective as a coercive measure.

Forty-seven percent felt that it was not that effective, while 30 percent felt that its efficacy as a compellent measure could not be determined.

Figure 3.5: Withdrawal From Indus Water Treaty

Description	Military	Academia	Journalist	Foreign Services
Effective	1	2	1	0
Not Effective	2	6	0	0
Not Certain	2	2	0	1

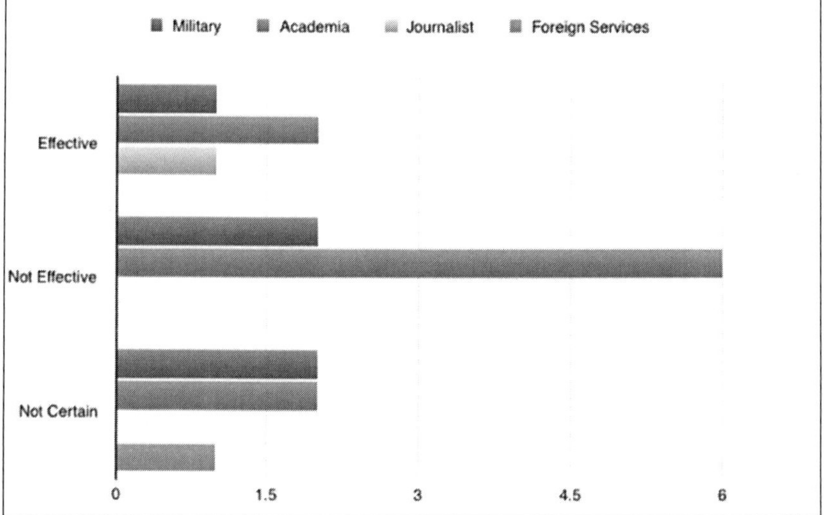

Revocation of Most Favoured Nation (MFN) Status

There was a unanimous view among the respondents that even if the MFN status was withdrawn, it would hardly make a dent in Pakistan's foreign trade as both the countries hardly have a trade relationship between them. Since the accordance of MFN status is an obligation under the World Trade Organization (WTO), it is highly unlikely that India would revoke MFN status.

Ivy League of Terrorism Speech at United Nations General Assembly (UNGA)

India's singling out of Pakistan as the terror hub of the world and raising the bogey of Balochistan has been considered as an important compellent measure, considering the growing economic and political clout of India at world forums. While some respondents feel that this speech and the one given by Mrs Sushma Swaraj, Minister of External Affairs at the UNGA[48] are a part of the tit-for-tat procedure used by both India and Pakistan at international platforms, some are of the opinion that this is an important coercive measure. Overall, 18 percent of the respondents felt that the UN speech was an important coercive measure while 29 percent felt that it was not. A huge majority, that is, 53 percent were not certain of the impact of the 'Ivy League of Terrorism' speech[49] as a coercive or compellent measure; though the second order effects were appreciated.

Figure 3.6: UN Speech

Description	Military	Academia	Journalist	Foreign Services
Effective	1	2	0	0
Not Effective	1	2	1	1
Not Certain	3	6	0	0

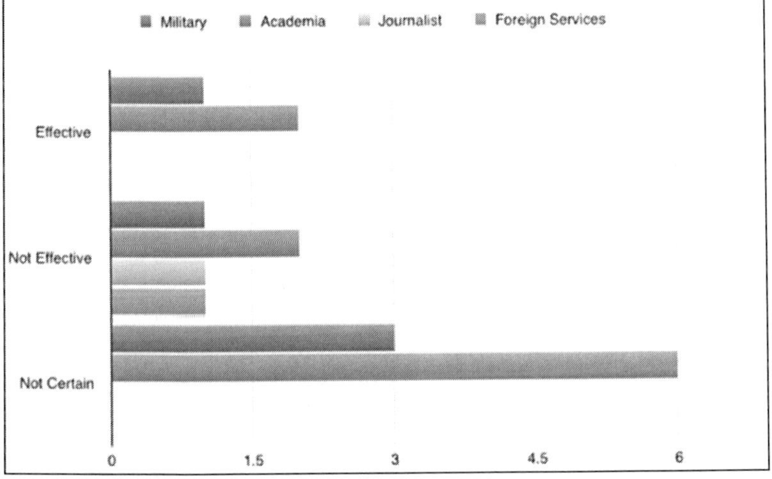

48. The Hindu, "Text of Sushma Swaraj's speech at U.N. General Assembly," [online] *The Hindu,* (2017).http://www.thehindu.com/news/resources/text-of-sushma-swaraj-speech-at-un-general-assembly/article19746157.ece
49. Nikhila Nataranjan, "Who Coined 'Ivy League of Terrorism' and how India found Language of Rebuttal against Pak," [online] *Firstpost,* (2016). https://www.firstpost.com/world/who-wrote-ivy-league-of-terrorism-rebuttal-against-pak-3016626.html

4

Efficacy of Coercive Diplomacy Measures Taken against Pakistan and Critical Analysis of Options Available

Options Available Post Uri

A number of actions were proposed and analysed post the Uri attacks including the now-famous surgical strikes across the LoC. The following table gives out the measures available to the Indian government in the aftermath of the Uri attacks:

Ser. No	Options Available	Type of Option
(a)	Issuing of demarches and statements to Pakistan; ask for an investigation	Political
(b)	Downgrade relations with Pakistan; recall Indian High Commissioner from Islamabad	Political
(c)	Influencing world opinion	Political
(d)	Introduction of UN General Assembly (UNGA) resolution against Pakistan asking for a resolution to condemn cross-border terror	Political
(e)	Raise the issue of Human Rights Violations (HRVs) in Balochistan at United Nations	Political
(f)	Close all trade channels (formal and informal) with Pakistan	Economic
(g)	Ban all Pakistani imports to India	Economic
(h)	Appeals to other countries to reduce trade with Pakistan	Economic
(j)	Ask for UN sanctions against Pakistan	Economic
(m)	Cross-border fire assaults	Military
(n)	Commando Raids on terror camps in PoK	Military
(o)	Air strikes against terror camps in PoK	Military
(p)	Targeted assassinations of individual leaders of terror groups	Military

Chronology of Compellent Steps taken by India

A study of the compellent steps taken by India in the aftermath of the Uri attacks showcases the sheer breadth of measures and options available with India in all the realms if taken to their logical conclusion. Following are the steps tha were taken by India against Pakistan after the Uri attacks:

Date of Compellent Actions Initiated/ Announced	Compellent Actions Taken/ Initiated	Initiated by (Agency/Actor)	Intended Audience	Intended Effect	Whether Long/ Medium/Short Term	Type of Measure
September 20, 2016	US Senator Ted Poe and Dana Rohrabacher (both Republican) introduce the Pakistan State Sponsor of Terrorism Designation Act 2016.[!]	US Congress, with covert and overt support and nudging from Taranjit Sandhu, Chargé d'Affaires at the Indian Embassy in Washington DC[@]	Pakistani government, governments of other nations, Pakistani Army and Indian public	Stop treating Pakistan as major non-North Atlantic Treaty Organization (NATO) ally and stop the flow of funds in terms of aid and reparations; isolate Pakistan on the world stage.	Long term	Political (primary) and financial (secondary)

Date of Compellent Actions Initiated/ Announced	Compellent Actions Taken/ Initiated	Initiated by (Agency/Actor)	Intended Audience	Intended Effect	Whether Long/ Medium/Short Term	Type of Measure
September 20, 2016	India announces consideration of asylum application of Brahamdagh Bugti, leader of Balochistan Republican Party (BRP)[#]	Ministry of External Affairs (MEA)	Pakistani Army, the Pakistani government and the United Nations	Raise the bogey of Baloch insurgency and possible secession from the Pakistani mainland in case a proxy war inside Indian administered Kashmir is not stopped.	Medium to long term	Political
September 20, 2016	The announcement that the Indian Army reserved the right to respond and would do so at the time and place of its choosing[$].	Indian Army	Pakistani Army	Intimidate Pakistani Army into stopping cover fire for infiltrating militants, forcing them to be more cautious.	Short term	Military

Date of Compellent Actions Initiated/ Announced	Compellent Actions Taken/ Initiated	Initiated by (Agency/Actor)	Intended Audience	Intended Effect	Whether Long/ Medium/Short Term	Type of Measure
September 21, 2016	The deal for buying 36 Rafales in fly away condition from France cleared[96]	Ministry of Defence	Pakistani Army and the Pakistani government	Send a signal that India is expediting its defence modernisation plans and looking at all options for punitive responses against Pakistan	Medium term	Political (primary) and military (secondary)
September 22, 2016	Ivy League of Terrorism speech at the 71st session of the UNGA	India's Permanent Mission to the United Nations, MEA	The Pakistani government, governments of various countries, the United States and the United Nations	The diplomatic offensive against Pakistan at all international forums and isolate it diplomatically	Medium to long term	Political

Date of Compellent Actions Initiated/ Announced	Compellent Actions Taken/ Initiated	Initiated by (Agency/Actor)	Intended Audience	Intended Effect	Whether Long/ Medium/Short Term	Type of Measure
September 26, 2016	Chairing of Review Meeting of Indus Waters Treaty (IWT) along with a statement by M- Vikas Swarup that "blood and water cannot flow together"^	Prime Minister's Office (PMO) and MEA (Ministry of External Affairs)	Pakistani Army, the Pakistani government, Pakistani Business Community and Landowners.	Threaten Pakistan with even abrogation of IWT leading to famine-like conditions inside the country	Short term (rhetoric)/ Long term (actual implementation on the ground)	Political (primary) and financial (secondary)
September 26, 2016	Dynamic Posture on Line of Control (LoC)	Indian Army	Pakistani Army	Massive and Punitive retaliation and possible 'Salami Slicing' in Pakistan-occupied Kashmir (PoK) sector	Short term	Military

Date of Compellent Actions Initiated/ Announced	**Compellent Actions Taken/ Initiated**	**Initiated by (Agency/Actor)**	**Intended Audience**	**Intended Effect**	**Whether Long/ Medium/Short Term**	**Type of Measure**
September 27, 2016	Cancellation of Attendance in South Asian Association for Regional Cooperation (SAARC) Summit supported by Bangladesh, Bhutan and Afghanistan[&]	PMO and MEA	Pakistani Government, governments of various countries	Isolation of Pakistan in the world and in its neighbourhood particularly raise the threat of an unfriendly government in Afghanistan	Long term	Political
September 27, 2016	Sushma Swaraj speech at UNGA accusing Pakistan of HRVs in Balochistan and urging the world to isolate Pakistan*	MEA	Pakistani Government, World Bodies, the United States and United Nations	Raise the bogey of Baloch insurgency and possible secession from the Pakistani mainland in case proxy war inside Indian administered Kashmir not stopped	Medium to long term	Political

Date of Compellent Actions Initiated/ Announced	Compellent Actions Taken/ Initiated	Initiated by (Agency/Actor)	Intended Audience	Intended Effect	Whether Long/ Medium/Short Term	Type of Measure
September 29, 2016	Surgical strikes on terror camps across PoK**	Indian Army	Pakistani Government, World Government, United States, United Nations, Indian Public and Pakistan-based Terror Groups	Deterrence by Denial, that is, raise the tactical cost of infiltrating proxies across the LoC; also explore windows of opportunities between Proactive Strategy and Pakistan's full-spectrum deterrence	Short, medium and long term	Military (primary) and political (secondary)
September 29, 2016	Ban on Pakistani actors on working in India***	Indian Motion Pictures Producers Association (IMPPA)	Pakistani Public and Pakistani Government	Stop cultural exchanges and indirectly impact the youth	Short term	Cultural

Date of Compellent Actions Initiated/ Announced	Compellent Actions Taken/ Initiated	Initiated by (Agency/Actor)	Intended Audience	Intended Effect	Whether Long/ Medium/Short Term	Type of Measure
September 29–30, 2016	Evacuation of border villages in Jammu and Kashmir (J&K), Punjab and Rajasthan; high alerts sounded	MHA and State Governments	The Pakistani government, world government, Indian public and Pakistani Army	Raise the threat of war	Short term	Political
October 03, 2016	Review of Most Favoured Nation (MFN) status given to Pakistan as per World Trade Organization (WTO) obligations@@	PMO and Ministry of Finance	Pakistani Business Community	Stop even the minimal flow of formal and informal trade with Pakistan and also disallow Indian technical and managerial expertise to Pakistani businesses	Medium term	Political (primary) and financial (secondary)

Effectiveness of Compellent Actions Taken by India

A qualitative analysis of the compellent measures taken by India against Pakistan in the wake of the Uri attacks is important as maximum steps were taken by the Indian government only after this attack. India now has an inventory of steps that it can apply in various permutations and combinations to coerce Pakistan into accepting its demands of stopping cross-border terrorism. These steps varied in their duration, intensity and even the type of audience addressed. For the sake of analysis, these measures have been listed in the table above in a chronological fashion and also categorised by their types. Some steps had multiple-order effects but for this analysis, only the primary effects have been taken into consideration, though their other effects have also been mentioned. The compellent steps that India took in the aftermath are given as under:

Political Steps

The Indian government took the following political steps.

US Congressmen Ted Poe and Dana Rohrabacher (both Republican) Introduced the Pakistan State Sponsor of Terrorism Designation Act 2016

Just 2 days after the Uri attacks, on September 20, 2016, two US lawmakers, Congressmen Ted Poe and Dana Rohrabacher introduced a Bill in the US House of Representatives (HR 6069) called the Pakistan State Sponsor of Terrorism Designation Act 2016[50] which sought to single out Pakistan as a safe haven and a sponsor for international terrorism. This Bill was deemed important as Congressman Ted Poe was the Chairman of the House Subcommittee on Terrorism. Though this may not seem to be a compellent act on part of the Indian government, very few people are aware of the background mechanics of Taranjit Sandhu, Charge d'Affaires of the Indian Embassy in the United States who worked day and night and utilised all his contacts within the US Congress to table the Bill. Though the Bill did not gather any support within the Congress, the fact that the Bill was introduced in the Congress,

---

50. US Congressman Ted Poe, "Chairman Poe Introduces the Pakistan State Sponsor of Terrorism Designation Act," [online] (2016). https://poe.house.gov/2016/9/chairman-poe-introduces-the-pakistan-state-sponsor-of-terrorism-designation-act, accessed August 12, 2017.

especially at the behest of India, gave a very strong signal to Pakistan that further acts of aggression against India will be met with a strong response from the United States and will affect the massive amount of aid going into the rentier state.

India Announced Consideration of Asylum Application of Brahamdagh Bugti, Leader of Balochistan Republican Party

India had raised the issue of HRVs by Pakistani security forces in Balochistan in many international forums as well as domestic ones. However, post the Uri attacks, this step of announcing consideration of asylum application of Brahamdagh Bugti, leader of the secessionist group Balochistan Republican Party (BRP) was a signal to Pakistan that India had more than a sympathetic ear to the Balochi rebels.[51] This was a signal to Pakistan that the spectre of Balochi insurgency could also be raised by India if the cross-border attacks did not stop, with the potential of embroiling Pakistan's already beleaguered armed forces further. However, the flip side of this is that the Balochis are not that well-armed and there is heavy infighting between the various factions. Also, Pakistani Army has effectively utilised the paranoia of Baloch insurgency supported by India within the minds of the Pakistani public to effectively entrench itself.

Deal for buying 36 Rafales in Flyaway Condition from France Cleared

Though the deal was a long time in making, the timing of the finalisation of the deal[52] suggests that this was a signalling attempt to Pakistan that India was on track with its defence modernisation and would be making all efforts to widen the conventional gap. This also meant that the Proactive strategy was also on track and India's strategic restraint should not be treated as its weakness.

51. T. Correspondent, "Brahamdagh Bugti to seek Asylum in India," [online] *dawn.com,* https://www.dawn.com/news/1284917, accessed on October 2017.
52. Franz-Stefan Gady, "India's Air Force Interested in 36 More Rafale Fighter Jets From France," [online] *The Diplomat*, (2017). https://thediplomat.com/2017/08/indias-air-force-interested-in-36-more-rafale-fighter-jets-from-france/,accessed on December 2017.

Ivy League of Terrorism Speech at the 71st Session of the UNGA

The Indian Representative, Ms Eenam Gambhir, part of India's Permanent Mission to the UN, gave an eloquent speech at the 71st session of the UNGA[53] by comparing Pakistan as the hub of terrorism and its various cities as the Ivy League of Terrorism. She highlighted the support given by the Pakistani state to non-state actors which had committed acts of terror in the entire world. As part of India's diplomatic offensive, this speech was well received at the world body, in stark comparison to the dismal performance of then Premier Nawaz Sharif, whose parroted lines had only a few takers as evident by the almost empty hall. This unequal reception at the UN was a signal to Pakistan that it was on the verge of international isolation and India's further diplomatic overtures would help it push past that edge.

Chairing of Review Meeting of IWT along with Statement by Mr Vikas Swarup that "Blood and Water Cannot Flow Together"

The IWT is one of the few aces up India's sleeves through which it can really strangle Pakistan, especially its power centre Punjab which is heavily dependent on agriculture. However, for India to actually do that it will have to abrogate its part of the IWT, a deal which has been guaranteed by the World Bank. Doing so will lead to massive loss to India's credibility, a country which has been trying to project itself as a mature power and possible leader. The best plan of action, as of now, is to fully utilise the 20 percent of the Indus Waters authorised under the IWT, as well as make the optimum use of the three eastern rivers that are officially part of the Indian side as per the IWT. Abrogating the treaty will require massive infrastructural commitments and permanent storage facilities to store the excess water, as well as the chances of China doing the same to India as the source of all the Indus water is in Tibet. This is a very powerful coercive measure if backed by a will to execute it to the terminal point. Signed in 1960 by then Prime Minister Jawaharlal Nehru and then Pakistan President Ayub Khan, the treaty allocates 80 percent of water from the six-river Indus water system to Pakistan. Beas, Ravi, Sutlej, Indus, Chenab and Jhelum from the Indus water system that

53. Nataranjan, n. 49.

flows from India to Pakistan. This is a unique treaty involving a third party. It was brokered by the World Bank.[54] India may face environmental damage if it decides to scrap the treaty, while Pakistan may face drought-like conditions. India is not in a position to stop or divert the water of the Indus River. It would take years of work to build huge dams or reservoirs or canals to change the flow of water. The move, however, may lead to floods in the valley. India cannot abrogate the treaty on a short notice. It takes years to divert the flow of a river. The government of India will have to prepare a long-term strategy if it intends to threaten Pakistan by diverting or stopping the water. Strategic issues expert Brahma Chellaney, recently wrote: "India should hold out a credible threat of dissolving the Indus Water Treaty, drawing a clear linkage between Pakistan's right to unlimited water inflows and its responsibility not to cause harm to its upper riparian."[55] The decision of not giving water to Pakistan may further enrage the terror elements in the country, making them intensify their attacks on India. Even the construction works for diverting the flow of water would be on the target of terrorists all the time. To check them, India will have to deploy huge security forces. This would further drain the Indian economy. About 65 percent of the area of Pakistan, including the entire Punjab province, is a part of the Indus basin. Interestingly, Pakistan boasts of the world's largest canal irrigation system because of its development of the basin, which covers over 90% of the irrigated area. The water from the Indus is important for the country for irrigation, drinking and other purposes. India's decision to abrogate the treaty would affect Pakistan severely. India's decision to abrogate the treaty may be detrimental to the country's interests in the long run. Experts say that people in Pakistan already do not like the fact that India controls its rivers, even as it has complied with the provision of the treaty sincerely. The Indian Express reports Shakil Ahmad Romshoo, head of the Earth Sciences Department, Kashmir University as saying: "In fact, the eagerness in a section of Pakistani society to

---

54. Mea.gov.in., "Indus Waters Treaty," [online] (1960). http://mea.gov.in/bilateral-documents.htm?dtl/6439/Indus accessed on August 21, 2017.
55. Brahma Chellaney, "Water Shortages could Trigger Asia Conflicts," [online] *Stagecraft and Statecraft,* (2017). https://chellaney.net/2017/12/31/water-shortages-could-trigger-asia-conflicts/, accessed on December 06, 2017.

wrest Kashmir originates in the desire to take control of its rivers. Any tinkering with the treaty is likely to see an intensification of Pak-backed activities in J&K."[56] According to Romshoo, Indus water cannot be stopped from flowing to Pakistan, unless India is ready to inundate its own cities. The Indian Express quotes Uttam Sinha of the Institute of Defence Studies and Analyses as saying that Pakistan can be pressured even without stopping the waters or violating any other provisions of the Indus Treaty.[57] "We have never used our rights on the western rivers. Under the Treaty, we can make use of the waters of the western rivers for irrigation, storage, and even for producing electricity, in the manner specified. If we just do what we are entitled to under the Treaty, it would be enough to send jitters through Pakistan. It would be a strong signal without doing anything drastic," Sinha said. According to Sinha, India needs to engage with Afghanistan on the development of the Kabul River that flows into Pakistan through the Indus basin. "This again can make Pakistan extremely nervous. It is in our strategic interest in any case to enhance our engagement on developmental issues with Afghanistan," he said. India, at present, enjoys a moral high ground because it respects all its treaties with the neighbouring countries. The decision to abrogate the treaty would make other smaller neighbours uneasy.[58] Not only would the neighbours be distrustful of India but also the country would not be in a position to say anything if China also takes a similar move against it. The country may also earn the ire of China. Indus originates in China and if the country decides to divert the Indus, India would lose over 35% of its river water. China is already building big dams on the Brahmaputra and it can hurt India's interests anytime. Not respecting the treaty may invite global condemnation to India as the treaty is an international agreement. At present, India is on

56. Shakil Ahmad Romshoo, "Assessing the Influence of Watershed Characteristics on the Flood Vulnerability of Jhelum Basin in Kashmir Himalaya," *Natural Hazards*, [online] https://www.researchgate.net/publication/277832264_Assessing_the_influence_of_watershed_characteristics_on_the_flood_vulnerability_of_Jhelum_Basin_in_Kashmir_Himalaya_reply_to_comment_by_Shah_2015, accessed on October 05, 2017.
57. Amitabh Sinha, "Turning off Indus Tap Easier Said than Done," [online] *The Indian Express,* (2016). http://indianexpress.com/article/explained/india-pakistan-relation-indus-water-treaty-terrorism-3044967/, accessed on October 20, 2017.
58. Ibid.

a moral high ground vis-à-vis Pakistan after the Uri attack. This would be lost if India does not follow the deal. Such decision by India would automatically bring World Bank in the picture and in support of Pakistan. The Kashmir issue will get a whole new dimension if India withdraws from the treaty. Not only this, it would trigger the formal beginning of water wars, which experts like Chellaney have been predicting for long. Moreover, it is unlike that Pakistan would mend its ways under Indian pressure of Indus water. There will also be spillover impacts due to India's withdrawal from the treaty on other countries. The first thing that India can do to showcase its seriousness is to start constructing run-of-the-river projects on those parts of the Indus which have been illegally contested by Pakistan and where there is a need for India to stamp its sovereignty. Steps, in this case, have already been taken and it is only a matter of time when India, without abrogating the IWT and just making the optimum use of whatever it has been accorded under the treaty, puts the squeeze on Pakistan. The Sawalkot Dam, one of such projects, was approved at a meeting held on February 20, 2017. Numerous other hydroelectric projects in J&K have been proposed by India, all of which faced objection from Pakistan due to the adverse impact it might have on that country. Islamabad fears the Sawalkot dam[59] will reduce the amount of water that flows through this water-stressed country. The Tulbul navigation project—a 439-feet-long, 40-feet-wide barrage to be constructed on the Jhelum river which would aid easy transport of commodities from Srinagar and Baramulla—was suspended when Pakistan claimed it was a violation of the IWT. Following the Uri attacks, the Indian government is also reviewing the Tulbul project with the aim of resuming work on it.[60] Islamabad says the flow of water into the Jhelum would be controlled by India and could result in droughts or floods in PoK. In a worst-case scenario, Pakistani analysts say multitudes of people will be affected due to the shortage of food, and productivity

59. Rosencranz, A. and Joseph, M, "By Building the Sawalkot Dam, is India Using Water as a Weapon against Pakistan?," [online] *The Wire,* (2017). https://thewire.in/external-affairs/sawalkot-dam-india-pakistan, accessed on October 2017.

60. Sameer Yasir, "Indus Waters Treaty, the Tulbul Project and its Implications on India-Pakistan relations—Firstpost," [online] *Firstpost,* (2016). https://www.firstpost.com/india/indus-waters-treaty-the-tulbul-project-and-its-implications-on-india-pakistan-relations-3022076.html, accessed on July 19, 2017.

will be extremely low, with water-intensive crops such as rice and cotton being deprived of water. Though consistent with the IWT, the Salal and Baglihar dams on the Chenab River are believed to have had a detrimental impact on Pakistan and now, with the setting up of the Sawalkot dam, India seems to be adding to Pakistan's apprehensions. As per the IWT, despite Pakistan's exclusive control over the western rivers, India can use the water from these rivers for domestic, nonconsumptive, agriculture and hydropower-generation purposes. With the treaty permitting India to use 3.6 million acres for storage facilities, an option that India has not used until now, Pakistan cannot prevent the construction of the Sawalkot dam.

Cancellation of Attendance in South Asian Association for Regional Cooperation Summit Supported by Bangladesh, Bhutan and Afghanistan

India, for the first time, cancelled its attendance to a SAARC Summit, citing the prevailing insecurity in the region as a reason. SAARC had been hijacked due to the rivalries between the two nuclear-armed rivals in the past too but India had always made attempts to stall the conduct of the event rather than an outright refusal to attend. Seeing India's stance and ensuring that the reason for the failure of the event does not fall on India's shoulders alone, Bangladesh, Bhutan and Afghanistan also pulled out of the summit. The show of strength in India's favour shows Pakistan that India is still a power to reckon with, however, may Pakistan try to hyphenate India with itself. Also, India's dreams of a SAARC minus Pakistan has been given an impetus with this show of hands in the 2016 summit as India plans to unveil a number of incentives for the SAARC nations including motor vehicle movement agreement, railway linkages, and the SAARC satellite programme for which all SAARC countries apart from Pakistan have signed up. As Afghanistan is landlocked, a separate 'air corridor' for cargo has been discussed.[61] India, in an effort to isolate Pakistan in the South Asian neighbourhood has also invented a host of bilateral and multilateral initiatives such as

61. Suhasini Haider, "Mission 'SAARC minus Pakistan'," [online] *The Hindu,* (2016). http://www.thehindu.com/news/national/Mission-%E2%80%98SAARC-minus-Pakistan%E2%80%99/article15005693.ece, accessed on September 23, 2017.

South Asia Sub-regional Economic Cooperation which is the grouping of India, Bangladesh, Bhutan, Maldives, Nepal, and Sri Lanka, Bay of Bengal Initiative for Multi-Sectoral Technical and Economic Cooperation (BIMSTEC) and so on. However, none of these groupings has managed to go beyond the regional niceties into something concrete either politically or financially. This measure has not had much of an impact on Pakistan as Pakistan was never beholden to India or the other South Asian nations for its trade or aid requirements. Politically, siding of Bangladesh with India has hurt its attempts to incite extremism in the country and Afghanistan's standing up on India's behalf has left Pakistan with a huge doubt over its Afghanistan strategy.

Sushma Swaraj Speech at UNGA Accusing Pakistan of HRVs in Balochistan and Urging the World to Isolate Pakistan

Minister of External Affairs, Mrs Sushma Swaraj's speech at the UNGA post the Uri attacks was a great coercive measure as it referenced the atrocities carried out by the Pakistani armed forces against the Baloch civilians. This equivalence to the Nawaz Sharif speech of atrocities by the Indian armed forces in Kashmir attempted two simultaneous steps: the first one was to relatively trivialise the Kashmir issue by comparing it with Balochistan and secondly, by comparing Balochistan to the Kashmiri 'freedom struggle',[62] it gave India full latitude to send men and materiel ala Pakistan to Baloch insurgents, if it wanted to. By harping on the HRVs in Balochistan, India sent a very strong signal to Pakistan. This would have been an important signal and an effective compellent measure had India displayed intent to follow through. In another case, the visa application of another high profile Baloch activist Naela Quadri Baloch was declined by India. Also, as of date, Brahamdagh Bugti's asylum application has been put on hold indefinitely and is in the process of being 'examined'.[63]

62. The Hindu, "Text of Sushma Swaraj's speech at U.N. General Assembly," [online] *The Hindu,* (2017).http://www.thehindu.com/news/resources/text-of-sushma-swaraj-speech-at-un-general-assembly/article19746157.ece, accessed on October 03, 2017.
63. dawn.com, "Brahamdagh Bugti to seek asylum in India," [online] *Dawn,* (2017). https://www.dawn.com/news/1284917, accessed on September 07, 2017.

Evacuation of Border Villages in Jammu and Kashmir (J&K), Punjab and Rajasthan; High Alerts Sounded

The evacuation of villages within 10 km of the International Border (IB) in the states of Punjab, Rajasthan and J&K and by sounding out high alerts, India sent out a strong and clear message to Pakistan that it was preparing for war. This was reminiscent of the Op Parakram mobilisation and led to the scrambling of aircraft by the PAF on their side of the IB. It also led to some unfortunate statements on the Pakistani side when one of their ministers threatened to nuke India with TNWs. Overall, the impact of this step was lost on the Pakistanis.

Review of MFN Status Given to Pakistan as per World Trade Organization (WTO) Obligations

In the year prior to Uri, that is 2015/16, India's total trade was worth $641 billion. Out of this huge amount, only $2.67 billion worth of goods were exported to Pakistan, forming 0.83 percent of India's export while less than $500 million or 0.13 percent were imported from that country. According to the MFN principle of the WTO's General Agreement on Tariffs and Trade (GATT)—to which India is a signatory/contracting party—each of the WTO member countries should "treat all the other members equally as 'most-favoured' trading partners." The WTO says, "Grant someone a special favour (such as a lower customs duty rate) and you have to do the same for all other WTO members."[64] Hence, though MFN sounds like special treatment, in effect it means nondiscrimination. The MFN status was accorded to Pakistan in 1996 as per India's commitments as a WTO member. But Pakistan has not reciprocated, reportedly citing 'non-tariff barriers' erected by India as well as a huge trade imbalance. According to the WTO's report on the Trade Policy Review of Pakistan (in 2015), "Pakistan is in the process of offering India Non-Discriminatory Market Access" (similar to MFN). Even if India withdrew the MFN status from Pakistan, there would not have been any significant trade fallout as the level of bilateral trade

64. Wto.org, "WTO|Understanding the WTO—What is the World Trade Organization?," [online] *World Trade Organization,* (n.d.). https://www.wto.org/english/thewto_e/whatis_e/tif_e/fact1_e.htm, accessed on June 15, 2017.

is 'very low'. Though it will have only a 'symbolic' impact in trade terms, politically it could result in India losing goodwill in the South Asian region, where it enjoys a trade surplus and is a party to a free trade pact called South Asian Free Trade Area, which also includes Pakistan. The move may also not go down well at the WTO-level. India could consider making use of a 'security exception' clause—Article 21(b)(iii)—in the GATT to deny the MFN status to Pakistan or bring in certain trade restrictions. According to a paper by Shailja Singh of the Centre for WTO Studies at the Indian Institute of Foreign Trade, "GATT and WTO practice shows that the countries have by and large observed self-restraint in using the national security exception.[65] This is hardly surprising as national security is too sensitive a subject that countries will be comfortable submitting to an international review." On the other hand, this move, if pushed through could have been seen as part of a new more assertive India which linked its economic policies to its national security.

Military Measures

Announcement that the Indian Army Reserved the Right to Respond and Would Do So at the Time and Place of Its Choosing

After the devastating attack on Pathankot and Uri, the Indian armed forces and especially the Indian Army have announced that they reserve the right to respond and would respond at the time and place of their choosing. This is a huge compellent measure although considering India's exclusive nonuse of the military option post Mumbai, the signalling looked weak at the time. A huge advantage of using this strategy was keeping Pakistan on tenterhooks as to the method and quantum of response that India would apply. A major reason for keeping this uncertainty factor was replicating Pakistan's calculated uncertainty about using its TNWs. Another reason was to keep the Pakistani army cautious and thereby reduce the incidents of infiltration, at least in the short term. One major drawback was that after this announcement,

65. Shailja Singh, "Protecting India's trade interests, [online] *The Hindu,* (2016). http://www.thehindu.com/opinion/columns/world-view-column-protecting-indias-trade-interests/article8194376.ece, accessed on November 14, 2017.

India had to respond by force, even if it was to satisfy public desire for revenge. India could not back down, for this would have meant a huge loss of credibility, both domestically and internationally. India had a number of options including air strikes, targeted assassinations, commando raids, salami slicing across PoK and shallow conventional thrusts across the IB, each with its own pros and cons.

Surgical Strikes on Terror Camps across PoK

The surgical strikes or enhanced commando raids that took place across the LoC at various launchpads of terror groups by para commandos of the Indian Army on the night September 28/29, 2016 were a response to the brutal killing of 18 soldiers in Uri on September 18, 2016.[66] These have served as the biggest coercive measure against Pakistan in the recent history and the public denial of Pakistani Army regarding the authenticity of the raids was a proof that the Pakistani Army had accepted the reality and could not, for the sake of their own existence, accept that the raid had taken place. Also, this strike was an attempt to test the waters by India and a step forward to call Pakistan's bluff about its 'irrationality'. With aggressive military strategies on both sides closing the window of opportunity for conventional war and Pakistan in the past getting away with proxy wars against the Indian mainland under the garb of the 'nuclear overhang', this strike has sent a signal that India has also devised a way to punish Pakistan and keep the conflict from going anywhere near nuclear. Though this action can be considered in the realm of tactical action, the implications for Pakistan are strategic.

Addressing Multiple Actors

As is clear from the table and the steps enumerated above, the measures that the Indian government took against Pakistan suffered from two major problems. First, since the steps taken were in multiple domains, there was a need to simultaneously address multiple forums inside Pakistan. While some were aimed solely at the Pakistani military,

66. Nitin A. Gokhale, "The Inside Story of India's 2016 'Surgical Strikes'," [online] *The Diplomat,* (2017). https://thediplomat.com/2017/09/the-inside-story-of-indias-2016-surgical-strikes/, accessed on November 18, 2017.

some addressed the business community and even the middle class of Pakistan itself. There was also a major chasm of opinion within India's strategic community, policymakers and within the political spectrum. Coordinated signalling or attempting to portray a united front took a major hit when parties in opposition started voicing their doubts about the veracity of the surgical strikes. Second, neither any assurances were conveyed publicly or privately nor some kind of a timeline had been set. The most important difference between deterrence and compellence is that of a timeline. While deterrence can afford to be timeless in nature, compellence has to function in a manner that stipulates deadlines.

Analysis of Options Available to India in Case of Future Attacks

In case of a future attack on an Indian garrison in the future and keeping in mind the above options exercised by India, some taken to their conclusion while some remaining open-ended, a critical analysis of the major steps is required. Following are the steps that would require an in-depth analysis:

Proactive Strategy

A brief background on the concept of Cold Start or Proactive Strategy is required before starting with its detailed analysis. The existing Holding and Strike Corps were reorganised into a more nimble structure. The defensive Holding Corps would become Pivot Corps which would be able to undertake limited offensives from defensive positions to create a shallow bridgehead into Pakistani territory. The objective was to be ready to retaliate into Pakistani territory within just a few days of a precipitating terror attack in India. To avoid risks of triggering Pakistani nuclear retaliation, the Indian forces would be designed and ordered to penetrate only 'short' distances into Pakistani territory, 10–15 km or more along the IB, perhaps deeper in the desert.[67] With a quick mobilisation and some element of surprise, Indian forces could gain and hold Pakistani territory before outside actors could pressure both governments to pull back.[68] Indian forces would hold captured territory

67. Walter C. Ladwig III, "A Cold Start for Hot Wars? The Indian Army's New Limited War Doctrine," *International Security* vol. 32, no. 3, 2007, pp.158–190.
68. Perkovich and Dalton, n. 5.

as leverage in subsequent negotiations to compel Pakistani authorities to genuinely and effectively uproot the groups conducting terrorism against India or Indian forces could withdraw after having taught Pakistani authorities a lesson sufficiently punitive to motivate them to eschew future attacks on India.

Issues

- Give an excuse to Pakistan to invest more extensively into battlefield nuclear weapons by referring to the existential threat being posed by India.
- A secondary aim of destroying the war-waging potential is a subjective one. As per Fred Ikle, inflicting punishment on the enemy nation is not only an ineffective strategy for ending a war; it may well have side effects that actually hasten the defeat of the side that relies on a strategy.
- Calibrating punishment is a significant challenge. Tit-for-tat as a strategy works in game theory but social psychology indicates that punitive actions have greater-than-intended effects on the recipient. Too little punishment will not inflict sufficient costs on Pakistan while too much punishment might lead to escalation.
- In the case of holding Pakistani land hostage as a bargaining chip for negotiations, foremost among them being to stop cross-border terrorism, topology and the population density of Pakistan are important. Relatively flat and unpopulated desert territory across the IB in Rajasthan would be easier to seize and hold for the Indian forces. But the staying capability of the Indian forces would be severely degraded by being subjected to insurgent attacks. This would also lead to an increase in recruitment among militants in Pakistan, Afghanistan and elsewhere to fight the occupiers and mount terrorist attacks in Kashmir and the Indian heartland.
- In case the Indian army is able to degrade and destroy the war-waging potential of the Pakistani army, then the capability of the Pakistani army to rein in militant groups and take action against them will be severely degraded.

Air Power

Limited punitive strikes would put India into a league with the United States and Israel as hard and militarily capable democracies determined to combat terrorism and to punish states that do not fulfil their obligations to curtail terrorist operations. Responding with airpower first would enable India to carefully calibrate its responses to terrorist attacks and ensure escalation dominance.[69] Just and proportionate air strikes would serve as a shot across the bow that would place the onus of further escalation on the enemy. Their high level of optical visibility serves to dramatically and emphatically highlight that such terrorist attacks are not acceptable any more. At the same time, airpower does not hold ground or capture territory. To that extent, its initial use may be less of an existential threat to Pakistanis than a full-fledged ground assault that captures and holds territory.

Issues

- The major issue would be to determine whether airstrikes would be conducted against targets in Kashmir or in the Pakistani heartland of Punjab and Sindh. If Pakistan retaliated by expanding the conflict beyond Kashmir, India would then be seen as justified in mounting wider operations in Pakistan.
- Attacking targets in Kashmir with airpower would be somewhat escalatory. It would also signal a measure of restraint, as compared with attacking targets in Pakistan's two eastern provinces. Attacking targets in PoK would convey an Indian interest in meting out visible punishment against Pakistan, which could satisfy Indian public opinion and political imperatives for the government.
- Indian air attacks on the Pakistani heartland would be much more punitive and provocative. Such attacks could reinforce the compellence message Indian leaders would wish Pakistan to receive. This could motivate Pakistani decision makers to act more decisively against terrorist groups, as India wants.
- Alternatively, attacking the heartland could cause Islamabad to fight back more intensively to defy New Delhi and signal that Pakistan could not be coerced.

69. Perkovich and Dalton, n. 5.

- If India (or other governments' intelligence agencies) did not have unmistakable proof that the leaders of Pakistan authorised the initial terrorist attack, an asymmetry in responsibility could be perceived. Pakistani leaders and society could feel that their homeland was being attacked unjustifiably—an act of aggression rather than of retaliation in self-defence. This would create a strong motivation for Pakistan to respond militarily, opening the way to cycles of escalation.
- There would be a challenge in addressing the types of targets: camps, leaders or state targets. Each presents its own set of challenges in terms of mobility, location, intelligence and provocation/nuisance value, among many others.
- The Indian Air Force would need to contend with Pakistani air defences if strikes were to be delivered by Indian aircraft operating in Pakistani airspace. There is a risk of Indian aircraft being shot down leading to the spectacle of wrecked Indian aircraft and dead or captured Indian pilots.
- India could also use cruise missiles to strike the same targets but the use of cruise missiles or otherwise could set a dangerous new precedent in Indo-Pakistan conflict.
- Air strikes cannot be one-time affairs as there would be an expectation on own side and a perception on the Pakistani side that the air strikes would either be followed by ground invasion or there would be a need to ready the ground forces once the air strikes go in, to stall a ground reaction from the other side.

Covert Operations

In a February 2014 lecture, 3 months prior to his appointment as the National Security Advisor, Ajit Doval proffered a subtle coercion idea, without the threat of conventional operations against Pakistan. He suggested that Pakistan should be made to understand: "You can do one Mumbai and you may lose Balochistan." Covert operations are clandestine actions that states take to undermine the interests of opponents in lieu of normal diplomatic or military action. Covert operations may or may not involve the use of force. They are a form of coercion and interference in another state's internal affairs that the perpetrator will deny having conducted. Covert operations are attractive as an alternative to 'doing nothing' to deter or retaliate against an adversary and 'doing too much'. Covert operations that involve the armed forces of a particular state are covert in the sense that they rely on stealth and secrecy and tend to involve relatively small units that enter and depart from foreign territory quickly.

Issues

- Covert operations may be undertaken by India to deter/disrupt the Pakistani terrorist groups from conducting major attacks on India and to diminish recruitment of new terrorists and to create incentives for the Pakistani security establishment to act decisively to prevent future terrorist attacks against India.
- Targeting individuals for attacks raises complicated legal, political and strategic issues beyond the physical challenges of identifying, tracking and striking the intended target. It is illegal to kill individuals on other states' territories during peacetime. Politically, the state's conduct of assassinations can be expected to produce heated political and legal debate. Strategically, the killing of individuals in other states may invite reciprocation from the state in which the killing occurred and/or from other states and sympathisers. Such killings are also known to stimulate recruitment of new personnel into terrorist ranks.
- Locating particular individuals and facilities and establishing their involvement in terrorism with confidence is difficult. Decision-makers of the attacking state must establish criteria for the level of confidence they require in the identification of a potential target and the amount of collateral damage in lives and property that they deem appropriate to risk inflicting in order to strike a target.
- Another issue is of timing. If India sought the element of surprise by striking individuals and support facilities before another major attack in India, the perpetrators and their supporters in Pakistan probably would make themselves much harder to target. Yet, if India sought the element of surprise by striking individuals and support

facilities before another major attack on India, Pakistanis and the wider world would be more likely to see India as an aggressor.

- The Indian authorities ordering the covert operations would have to determine whether targeting anti-India terrorists on Pakistani territory would motivate Pakistani authorities to change their policies.

Non-violent Compellence

This has been India's forte and was used to the hilt in the aftermath of Uri and Pathankot attacks. India's effective use of campaigning at the UN and other multilateral forums ensured that Pakistan was pressured by the United States and even China to control its non-state actors and make all attempts to eliminate them. Recognising that the UN Security Council (UNSC) is not the most plausible vector for mobilising and channelising power, India could still use the obligations set out by UN resolutions such as 1373 as the basis for pressing states bilaterally and regionally to hold Pakistan to account. India's power to influence other key states will increase as its economy grows. Military modernisation, as reforms are implemented, will enable India to project greater power in its region and beyond, adding to its international leverage.[70] The following measures can be used by India to compel/coerce Pakistan to comply with its demands.

Economic Sanctions

The results of economic sanctions historically have been mixed. A classic study by Hufbauer, Schott and Elliott in 1990[71] concluded that economic sanctions were effective approximately one-third of the time. A recent comprehensive study suggests that the target state's membership in international institutions and the imposition of harsh economic costs are the factors most positively correlated with sanctions' effectiveness. The most effective and rarest sanctions are those imposed on a global basis under authorisation by the United Nations. Pakistan is, paradoxically, less vulnerable to economic sanctions than it might seem. The country's gross domestic product (GDP) in dollars at the official exchange rate was

70. Daniel Markey, "Complex U.S.-Pakistan Relations," *Council on Foreign Relations,* (2017).
71. Gary Clyde Hufbauer et al., *Economic Sanctions Reconsidered,* 3rd ed. (Peterson Institute for International Economics, 2009).

estimated in 2014 to be $246.9 billion. The GDP ranking in the world is 174. The Pakistani economy depends significantly on remittances from workers abroad, International Monetary Fund (IMF) support, aid from the United States and project funding from China. Pakistan's political economy is so troubled, so fails to create conditions for giving young people confidence in their secular future, and is so dependent on international assistance that the states that provide this assistance are highly reluctant to cut it off. A more effective tactic, that of targeting the Pakistani state indirectly, would be to persuade the IMF to assess how risks of major terrorism emanating from Pakistan against India would affect Pakistan's capacity to make future required payments to the IMF. Indian officials could persuade the staff at IMF to increase the salience of the counterterrorism agenda by raising these questions. Discussing these issues would add uncertainty to the calculations of particular investors in Pakistan, strengthening incentives for the government to demonstrate its commitment to prevent terrorism.

United States, China and Security Assistance to Pakistan

Beijing can and most likely would veto any effort to adopt UN sanctions on Pakistan. India could still urge others to raise the issue in the United Nations, if only to shine an international spotlight on China's unwillingness to penalise a state that was once again associated with a major terrorist attack on India, notwithstanding China's own concerns about terrorism. Also, China is Pakistan's leading source of imports and its second largest export market (behind the United States). China has the strategic motivation and resources to provide substitute aid and financing to Pakistan in the event that other sources cut them off. The United States is Pakistan's biggest export market and, with one interruption, has long been its greatest source of economic and military aid. According to data provided by Pakistan's Board of Investment, US assistance accounts for 22 percent of all foreign investment into Pakistan between 2007 and 2015.[72] There is literally no prospect of effective economic sanctions on Pakistan if the United States does not participate. Distinctions are

72. Tradingeconomics.com, "Pakistan Foreign Direct Investment|2010–2018|Data|Chart| Calendar," [online] *Trading Economics,* (2018). https://tradingeconomics.com/pakistan/foreign-direct-investment, accessed on January 02, 2018.

made between economic and security assistance to Pakistan. Not many argue for the stoppage of the former which is required to sustain human capability in the country. But as the beneficiaries of the latter are the Pakistani army and its intelligence agencies, who are responsible for cultivating groups such as the LeT and Haqqani Network, the argument is to deny the benefits in the future if it does not demonstrably act to prevent further violence against Indian and American interests in Afghanistan and India. If India could muster support in the United States for cutting security assistance and support in the European Union, Japan and Australia for curtailing economic assistance, this could raise the cost of the Pakistani security establishment's unwillingness to demobilise anti-India groups. The strategy would be to make Pakistan appeal to China for greater assistance to make up for any amount and type of aid that was being withdrawn by the United States and others. If Beijing assented, then China would feel more acutely the burden of carrying Pakistan. This could strengthen China's interests in urging Pakistani leaders to take actions in the counterterrorism domain that would limit China's exposure to Pakistani risk.

Political Isolation

Pakistan is fundamentally open to the international community. By persuading other states to clarify that they would politically and socially condemn and, where appropriate, isolate Pakistan in the event of another major attack on India, Indian officials and civil society leaders could buttress those in Pakistan who do not want their state to be associated with terrorism. The August 2015 Joint Statement by the Governments of India and the United Arab Emirates is a model that India could seek to induce other states to emulate. This statement denounced "terrorism in all forms and manifestations, wherever committed and by whomever, calling on all states to reject and abandon the use of terrorism against other countries, dismantle terrorist infrastructures where they exist, and bring perpetrators of terrorism to justice." Many in Pakistan correctly perceived that this language was directed at their country, and saw it as an example of Indian soft power eroding Pakistan's standing in a country—the United Arab Emirates —that is important to Pakistan.

Conclusion and Recommendations

The previous chapter analyses in detail the various measures taken by the Indian government against Pakistan in the aftermath of the Uri attacks. Uri has been taken as a case study and stands as a symbol for attacks against all other garrisons, as this is the incident in which India unleashed a multidirectional and potent diplomatic and military offensive. After conducting exhaustive and extensive interviews, delving into the literature of Indo-Pakistan relations and the global literature on coercive diplomacy, following are the recommendations for India to practice successful coercive diplomacy in case of attacks on military garrisons in the future:-

Application of Specific Counterterrorism Sanctions

The UNSC has adopted specific sanctions that target individuals alleged to be involved in terrorism. UNSC Resolution 1267 was adopted in 1999 after the al-Qaeda attacks on the US embassies in Nairobi and Dar es Salaam. This resolution ordered states to freeze the assets of the Taliban for harbouring Osama bin Laden and his associates. These sanctions were expanded by Resolution 1333 in December 2000, directly targeting bin Laden and other al-Qaeda leaders. Thereafter, a mechanism for listing individuals and entities to be sanctioned under these resolutions was created. On this basis, in 2006 and 2008, the United States encouraged by India sought to place Hafiz Saeed and Jamaat-ud-Dawa, the parent organisation of LeT, on the list of individuals and entities to be sanctioned for having been involved in terrorist activities. China, however, imposed a technical hold on this move citing lack of evidence.[73] This case showcases the challenges involved in using non-violent means to target terrorists involved in incidents within India. Implementing sanctions on individuals requires the cooperation of

73. Press Trust of India, "China Extends Technical Hold on Masood Azhar's Terror Listing at the UN," [online] *Hindustan Times,* (2017). https://www.hindustantimes.com/world-news/china-extends-technical-hold-on-jem-chief-masood-azhar-at-the-un/story-2UWhREGfhF11gULeXIjuRK.html, accessed on September 16, 2017.

states in which they live and operate. Even if somehow these bodies are willing and able to prosecute suspected individuals and entities, the persuasive evidence is difficult to provide and acquire. Also, the biggest challenge for India lies in the ability to persuade other key states, especially China, to support further UN-based resolutions and initiatives to hold individuals, organisations and the state of Pakistan to account if future acts of terrorism are attributed to actors affiliated to Pakistan. India's leverage to press other states, however, has been growing in the past couple of years and India must keep up the diplomatic offensive at various multilateral forums to denounce Pakistan and influence other countries to support sanctions on the state.

Continuation of Talks

It has been seen that whenever India and Pakistan's political classes are on the verge of a breakthrough, there is a concerted attempt by the non-state actors and the powerful Pakistani military to derail them using proxies to attack targets in India. The trend has been by India to break off the talks and then ask for conditionalities to be fulfilled before starting with the talk again. This plays right into the hands of the lobby, especially the ISI and the ex-soldiers of the Pakistani Army that do not want normalised relations with India. Instead of breaking up talks, India must go through with the talks and insist on peace.

Coercion by Denial

Surgical strikes on terrorist launchpads across the LoC and their public declaration have ushered in a new era of Indian assertion. This trend needs to continue but should be based on tactical feasibility, operational readiness and strategic necessity, combined with political acumen. Surgical strikes should not be treated as crowd pleasers or as a form of vindictive tit for tat. These should be calibrated in order to be below the threshold of acute pain for Pakistan and be damaging enough to get the message across. The cost of Pakistan to attack garrisons inside India should be made so high each time these attacks are launched that a doubt is created inside its mind and it is forced to make a cost–benefit analysis every time it plans a strike inside Indian territory. The strikes did have a compellent element and the fact that Pakistani army is yet to accept that such strikes took place underscores that the logic of South Asian nuclear deterrent has been turned on its head.

Isolation at Multilateral Forums

Though many of the respondents interviewed for this dissertation were not very convinced that India had the ability to isolate Pakistan, they were looking at only the partial picture. It is quite true that India does not have the ability to directly isolate Pakistan but with its growing political and economic clout and its assertive foreign policy, India's ability to influence states such as the United States and bodies such as the European Union, United Nations, Gulf Cooperation Council has grown steadily. As this influence grows and that of Pakistan wanes, only to be supported by China, India will be able to influence the world opinion on its fight against the terror being exported by Pakistan in the form of cross-border proxies and also link it with the global war against terrorism. India, in the past, has been able to apply pressure on Pakistan through the use of these channels. Pakistan's traditional allies such as the United Arab Emirates and Saudi Arabia have been befriended by India and strong extradition and intelligence deals have been signed with them. This in itself acts as a coercion policy as it is a message to Pakistan that in spite of its emphasis on its Islamic character, India still holds a much important place within the members of the Gulf Cooperation Council and the broader Islamic world.

Indus Waters Treaty

Though the government's decision to announce publicly that it was going to look into the provisions of IWT as per the maxim that 'blood and water cannot flow together' was a step in the correct direction, there is a need to follow it up with more concrete steps. The work on Tulbul barrage[74] which had been stopped due to Pakistan's complaints needs to be restarted. India needs to utilise the maximum potential of its allotted 20 percent of the Western rivers by constructing and restarting work on various 'run-of-the-river' projects, especially in the state of J&K.

74. Chellaney, n. 55.

Use of Backchannels/Track II Diplomacy

India needs to shed the morality badge, a remnant of the Nehruvian era and start behaving according to the diktats of IR. There needs to be effective backchannels consisting of subject and domain experts and with enough empowerment and latitude by the government to initiate and proceed with negotiations with their Pakistani counterparts. This needs to be in the private domain and away from public scrutiny. The rhetoric of toughness and 'not ceding an inch' must be maintained in the public domain, while working the backchannels for a doable solution.

Nurturing of Strategic Culture

For coercive diplomacy to work there needs to be a supplementarity and complementarity between the military and the diplomatic channels to bring about the intended change in the adversary. Coercive diplomacy can only work if backed up by the threat of destructive force, with displays of force intended to portray the serious nature of the diplomacy sometimes. But it also needs to be remembered that coercive diplomacy is the use of all conduits short of the use of force. There is a debate that even the use of force constitutes coercive diplomacy. However, there is a need of a strategic culture within the country that knows how to blend diplomatic, political, economic and military means to present a unified front to the adversary and use carefully calibrated means to pressurise Pakistan to close its terror camps and then slowly demobilise the various terror groups acting on its behalf and operating from its soil. Unfortunately, since this culture is not present in India at the moment, there is a need to nurture this culture by linking the civil and military domain together. Various means can be utilised such as creating and empowering the institution of the Chief of Defence Staff.

South Asian Association for Regional Cooperation Minus Pakistan

The plan of empowering and integrating the SAARC nations and excluding Pakistan has been put on track but needs to be expedited. Initiatives such as motor vehicle movement agreements, railway linkages, air cargo corridors and launch of SAARC satellites are all measures that have benefits for all SAARC nations but exclude Pakistan. By showcasing the benefits that Pakistan is being deprived of, India needs to use its soft power in a big way to coerce Pakistan. However, India also needs to shed its 'Big Brother' image and begin to treat its neighbours in a more equitable manner or face the danger of these countries sliding into China's orbit.

Raising of Balochistan Issue at International Level

Raising of the Balochistan and even the Gilgit-Baltistan (GB) issue by India has troubled Pakistan at various international forums. China's China–Pakistan Economic Corridor (CPEC), whose major portion runs through the restive Balochistan province is also concerned about the safety of its workers, technicians and investments. India has managed to highlight the atrocities of the Pakistani armed forces in Balochistan at various forums, something which had been cleverly hidden by the Pakistanis and has finally achieved leverage. Also, the asylum applications of various Balochi leaders need to be considered and analysed to force Pakistan into conceding India's demands.

Conclusion

As this monograph is concluded, numerous things have come to light. India's track record of coercive diplomacy against Pakistan has been poor and has occurred in fits and starts. Most of the measures that have been taken have suffered from a mismatch between the political and diplomatic overtures on one hand and military manoeuvres on the other. India has always been shy of using its military advantage over Pakistan in order to coerce it into acceding to its demands. India has always been accused of 'punching below its weight' in IR. Whenever India suffered terrorist attacks at the hands of Pakistan-sponsored proxies, India has never been able to use a synergised approach to deal with Pakistan, instead using ad hoc methods that have been never fully successful. However, with the increase in attacks on Indian forces since 2013, India has had to calibrate its strategy of dealing with Pakistan. Especially post Uri attacks, India applied a variety of measures to force Pakistan to concede to its demands. Though not all steps taken were successful, the initial steps that have been taken need to be followed up and a strategic culture evolved which imbibes in the country an initiative to apply coercive diplomacy measures using the full might of the resources at its disposal

Appendix 'A'

Interview with Maj Gen Pramod Kumar Saighal (Retd), Defence Expert

Question 1. In terms of intermediate-level attacks such as Pathankot and Uri, the Government of India has taken ad-hoc steps to respond. These attacks are neither too small such as arms snatching, or killing of a few civilians to elicit more than a tactical response from the local security agencies, nor large enough 'defining' events such as Mumbai or the Parliament attacks for an Operation Parakram-like response. Attacks such as these fall in the middle of the spectrum but are significant in their own sense. Pathankot, as it came in the wake of similar attacks in Pakistan such as the Mehran Air Base or the Karachi Naval Base where two refurbished and state-of-the-art P3C Orions were destroyed and Uri, which occurred just 2 months after the Burhan Wani killings came in the wake of intense nationalist outcry on the social media and the fact that 19 Indian soldiers were killed, most of them being burnt to death than by enemy fire. Various options were considered by the Indian government such as reviewing the Indus Waters Treaty (IWT), the Most Favoured Nation (MFN) status of Pakistan, the conduct of surgical strikes, which were conspicuously absent in the aftermath of the Pathankot attacks. Do you think there is a need for a rulebook, maybe in terms of a defined National Security Policy to deal with such kind of events, where out of a host of options available to the Government, a number of permutations and combinations may be worked out to chalk out an adequate response to coerce Pakistan?

Answer 1. In International Relations, no two situations are generally similar, so no government can afford to have a rigid rulebook which lays down concrete options. On the other hand and more importantly, the shaping of the international environment is critical, to make a base for your further coercive actions. This is what the Modi government has been able to achieve, in the various diplomatic trips that Mr Modi went on. Set piece or preconceived solutions to any crisis may fail or misfire. In our case, the capability and capacity exist but the will is missing. Every year, the government is supposed to convey to the heads of the three services, the threat perception to the country. The three services will then tailor their preparedness to the threat perception. Since Independence, there has been no genuine effort by the government to convey the same to our forces. Also, the concept of jointness is just not there, neither within the armed forces nor in the various departments of the government to respond as part of a Comprehensive National Power. There is no understanding of the concept of war in the Ministry of Defence (MoD).

Question 2. Post Uri attacks, there was a lot of talk and rhetoric, especially in the media about 'isolating' Pakistan. Do you think, in today's scenario, that a state can isolate another state? What is the meaning of isolation in the international context?
Answer 2. I will answer this question in this manner. PM Modi defined terrorism at all the summits that he went to G20, Bay of Bengal Initiative for Multi-Sectoral Technical and Economic Cooperation (BIMSTEC), South Asian Association for Regional Cooperation (SAARC) and United Nations, to name a few. However, it was only when terror attacks started happening in the Western world did the Americans and the Europeans started taking notice and accepting terrorism as the greatest existential threat to the world. Pakistan came in the limelight as the hub of terrorism. In my view, the isolation of Pakistan has been accomplished to a large extent. Look at the indicators: the US and the Gulf Cooperation Council (GCC) have stopped the flow of funds to Pakistan, countries of the Organisation of Islamic Conference (OIC) have shut down safe havens of the terrorists and seized their assets.

Question 3. But, on the other hand, Russia continued with its planned exercise with Pakistan and still supplies and in fact has increased its delivery of lethal armaments to Pakistan. Your comments.
Answer 3. You have to look at this in the following manner: Russia has started supporting Pakistan to get the Americans into the quagmire of Afghanistan. That's why you see news reports of Taliban and allegedly al-Qaeda also being supported by the Russians against the Americans in Afghanistan.

Question 4. Do you think that Track II diplomacy works? Should it be used in conjunction with coercion or as a stand-alone part?
Answer 4. Track II diplomacy is always in place. Look at Musharraf's Four-point formula for the solution of the Kashmir dispute. Sir Creek and Siachen were also on the verge of resolution through Track II diplomacy, but the proposals were shot down at the last moment.

Question 5. Do you think that measures such as surgical strikes, threatening to revoke the MFN status or the IWT have had any compellent effect against Pakistan, to stop its cross-border infiltration and terrorism against India? Is there a need to look at incipient steps in a process or does the end state only matter?
Answer 5. Surgical strikes were meant to be a signal to the world audience that India is serious about its sovereignty. A visible effect of the post-surgical strike environment has been the shifting of terrorist camps in Pakistan and Pakistan-occupied Kashmir (PoK) near to Army cantonments and especially near heavily populated areas to make it costly for us to repeat the same thing, by incurring major collateral damage. High-profile leaders of groups such as Markaz-ud-Dawa or Lashkar e Taiba have been given protection of the Inter-Services Intelligence Directorate under the pretext of house arrest. Paradoxically, infiltration attempts and cease-fire violations have increased as against previously. Incidents of increased violence are signs of weakening Pakistan and increasing Indian determination rather than its increasing strength.

Question 6. What, according to you, are the coercive measures or steps that need to be taken in order to pressurise Pakistan to accede to our demand of stopping cross-border infiltration?
Answer 6. The answer lies in faultlines within the country; ethnical such as Balochistan or Sindh or between the majority Sunni and the minority Shia, Christian or the Sikh communities. These need to be exploited in a balanced manner with all the facets of diplomacy including coercion playing their part in a level manner. It is not in India's interests to initiate the disintegration of Pakistan.

Appendix 'B'

Interview with Lt Gen Philip Campose (Retd), PVSM, AVSM, Former General Officer Commanding in Chief Western Command, Vice Chief of Army Staff and Distinguished Fellow, Centre for Land Warfare Studies (CLAWS)

Question 1. In terms of intermediate-level attacks such as Pathankot and Uri, the Government of India has taken ad hoc steps to respond. These attacks are neither too small such as arms snatching, or killing of a few civilians to elicit more than a tactical response from the local security agencies, nor large enough 'defining' events such as Mumbai or the Parliament attacks for an Operation Parakram-like response. Attacks such as these fall in the middle of the spectrum but are significant in their own sense. Pathankot, as it came in the wake of similar attacks in Pakistan such as the Mehran Air Base or the Karachi Naval Base where two refurbished and state-of-the-art P3C Orions were destroyed and Uri, which occurred just 2 months after the Burhan Wani killings came in the wake of intense nationalist outcry on the social media and the fact that 19 Indian soldiers were killed, most of them being burnt to death than by enemy fire. Various options were considered by the Indian government such as reviewing the IWT, the MFN status of Pakistan, conduct of surgical strikes, which were conspicuously absent in the aftermath of the Pathankot attacks. Do you think there is a need for a rulebook, maybe in terms of a defined National Security Policy to deal with such kind of events, where out of a host of options available to the Government, a number of permutations and combinations may be worked out to chalk out an adequate response to coerce Pakistan?

Answer 1. There should be reference points within the system to guide policy but they must not be put in the public domain. The government cannot be held accountable with reference to those points nor must it be made to account in the context of those points. Measures like these cannot be quantified, as in there can be permutations and combinations but fixing those measures in response to a particular action or incident is not advisable. The best option is not to mention them at all. However, an inventory of possible steps can always be made, out of public domain, and pros and cons of all the possible steps such as limited war, missile strikes or air strikes must remain classified. Pakistan's requirements are sub-conventional and the actions initiated by them generally remain below our level of tolerance. Their rhetoric of use of nuclear threat against India is to deter us from engaging in proactive operations.

Question 2. Post Uri attacks, there was a lot of talk and rhetoric, especially in the media about 'isolating' Pakistan. Do you think, in today's scenario, that a state can isolate another state? What is the meaning of isolation in the international context?
Answer 2. It is not possible to isolate Pakistan. There are enough supporters of the country due to various strategic aims that preclude any chance of isolation, especially by us. For example, the creation of Pakistan was due to its future use as a base against communism. Over the last 2 years, Western powers have given Pakistan almost a thousand Armoured Personnel Carriers as part of Excessive Defence Articles, basically the leftovers of the Iraqi and Afghanistan missions. As of today, no one is interested in isolating Pakistan. OIC has not isolated Pakistan. However, OIC being friendly to India itself is a threat to Pakistan. When talking about the GCC, flow of funds to Pakistan has not stopped, in fact, Gen Raheel Sharif, the former Pakistani Army Chief has been made the head of the 'Islamic NATO', that is, the Saudi campaign against Yemen. The Americans have not stopped their aid package, just put a temporary halt. Historically also, the squeeze has never worked. Five or six months down the line, the funds will again be released. The issue is that the Indian military can implement nothing that the Americans ask and basically it's all talk. When you look at the travel program of the Indian Army Chief when he goes to the US, it's around 3 days give or take. But when the Pakistani Chief visits the US, it's generally around 15 days. American money is being used to support the Haqqani network which then is used to attack American soldiers in Afghanistan, so they are concerned with HQN. They are not much bothered by LeT or Hizbul Mujahideen as these groups are primarily India-focused. The relationship between Pakistan and the US

is much more stronger as compared to India. The NATO is dependent on Karachi, its lifeline for operations in Afghanistan. Almost 85 percent of the logistics support still comes through the port. Pakistan's lobbying at Capitol Hill is also much stronger than India's and it spends much more than us on lobbying efforts.

Question 3. Do you think that Track II diplomacy works? Should it be used in conjunction with coercion or as a stand-alone part?
Answer 3. Track II diplomacy may work in the form of backchannels. You need the same kind of people in both the bureaucratic as well as military channels so that a link is formed and both sides are working towards a common set of goals. One way of Track II diplomacy is the United Nations Peace Keeping Operations where militaries of both the countries work side by side. This, in the future, can be taken up in the form of joint headquarters and joint training in terms of Humanitarian Assistance and Disaster Relief or joint seminars. It's easier to interact with Pakistan when you imagine it as an independent country, but not as a Chinese proxy.

Question 4. Do you think that measures such as surgical strikes, threatening to revoke the MFN status or the IWT have had any compellent effect against Pakistan, to stop its cross-border infiltration and terrorism against India? Is there a need to look at incipient steps in a process or does the end state only matter?
Answer 4. I think that even scholarly articles published in think-tank journals can also act as a deterrent of sorts. As far as the IWT is concerned, the Indian government will never revoke it as it's underwritten by the World Bank. India hopes to be a major power in the future and certain behaviour is expected out of it, that's why the government will never do it. Even if we implement the treaty in letter and just stick to our side of the agreement, it will put a big squeeze on Pakistan, there is no need to go all the way and revoke the treaty. Fidayeen strikes on our camps gives us justification to have a publicly declared incoherent policy and that's the message that is needed to be conveyed to Pakistan. If you want to know whether we should look at steps or just the final result,

you must remember Operation TUPAC. If Pakistan is serious about stopping terrorism, has Pakistan stopped Operation Tupac? The bigger picture, according to me, is that Pakistan still seeks revenge for 1971 by utilising the resources and material during the Central Intelligence Agency's operations against the Soviets and now against the Taliban. If you look at the recent past, the Western nations have contributed almost a thousand APCs to Pakistan, enabling to effectively restructure its response to our Proactive Operations. As a result, our capability to compel it to do anything has decreased. Do we need to increase the military balance in our favour? Yes. Will we? No. Pakistan has picked up Huey Cobras from US allies and refurbished them. Its development of Tactical Nuclear Weapons and declared strategy of Full Spectrum Deterrence have ensured that Pakistan has achieved deterrence. Sadly, China, on one hand, has been dismissive of India's nuclear capability while Pakistan has used the claim of same to build up its conventional capability. The 'Beg Doctrine' by the then Chief of Army Staff of Pakistan Gen Aslam Beg, post Brasstacks, was introduced during the Zarb-e-Momin exercise to increase Pakistani Army's capability to absorb an Indian offensive and still launch a counteroffensive. India's Cold Start put him on the back foot and the situation remained the same till 2001 or more specifically 9/11. With a massive influx of aid, Pakistan reoriented its entire strategy of warfighting and heavily mechanised its forces reducing the advantage of our conventional edge. When the Mumbai attacks happened, the world and especially Pakistan was expecting us to do something, but we did not. There was a general perception that we had been frightened into complacence due to the nuclear factor. Pakistan also conducted the Azm-e-Nau series of exercises to retaliate against India's perceived 'Cold Start' strategy. After Azm-e-Nau II, the 'New Concept of War Fighting' was introduced to neutralise Indian Army's capability to gain success with Cold Start. The saving face for India has been Pakistan's western front as he is unable to sort that out. Also, increasingly better relations between India and Pakistan also put him in a fix. Our own capability, though comparatively reduced, is still better than Pakistan's and Pakistan's western border which has consumed almost 30 to 50 percent of his active duty forces, has acted as a deterrence as Pakistan can never be confident if terror strikes can be below India's threshold of tolerance. Also, there seems to be no point of reconciliation between the Pakistani Army and the Tehreek-e-Taliban Pakistan.

Question 5. What, according to you, are the coercive measures or steps that need to be taken in order to pressurise Pakistan to accede to our demand of stopping cross-border infiltration?

Answer 5. The basic thinking of the Pakistani 'Deep State' was that if the threshold of terror attacks were to be kept small, then India would not have any answer. However, the successful surgical strikes have proved that there is an answer. The Pakistanis were not even aware that India had conducted a surgical strike and when they found out, they used a denial strategy to prevent loss of face. Also, the surgical strikes were not considered serious enough to credit response or acceptance. This shows that there is a scope for something to happen.

Appendix 'C'

Interview with Lt Gen Gurmit Singh (Retd), PVSM, UYSM, AVSM, VSM, Former Adjutant General and Distinguished Fellow, Centre for Land Warfare Studies (CLAWS)

Question 1. In terms of intermediate-level attacks such as Pathankot and Uri, the Government of India has taken ad hoc steps to respond. These attacks are neither too small such as arms snatching, or killing of a few civilians to elicit more than a tactical response from the local security agencies, nor large enough 'defining' events such as Mumbai or the Parliament attacks for an Operation Parakram-like response. Attacks such as these fall in the middle of the spectrum but are significant in their own sense. Pathankot, as it came in the wake of similar attacks in Pakistan such as the Mehran Air Base or the Karachi Naval Base where two refurbished and state-of-the-art P3C Orions were destroyed and Uri, which occurred just 2 months after the Burhan Wani killings came in the wake of intense nationalist outcry on the social media and the fact that 19 Indian soldiers were killed, most of them being burnt to death than by enemy fire. Various options were considered by the Indian government such as reviewing the IWT, the MFN status of Pakistan, conduct of surgical strikes, which were conspicuously absent in the aftermath of the Pathankot attacks. Do you think there is a need for a rulebook, maybe in terms of a defined National Security Policy to deal with such kind of events, where out of a host of options available to the Government, a number of permutations and combinations may be worked out to chalk out an adequate response to coerce Pakistan?

Answer 1. I will first start with my perception of what constitutes coercive diplomacy. I believe there is a spectrum of dealing with states on an international level. If military or war constitutes one end of the spectrum, then diplomacy constitutes the other. In diplomacy, there are always two ways of looking at a problem. There is no such thing as zero diplomacy. On the other hand, if you see, the MoD takes the military for granted while the Ministry of External Affairs interacts directly with the armed forces. There is a reversal of roles here. The entire world is living in an arena of coercive diplomacy. In layman's terms, it is handling an incident or a situation that does not take you to war. Coercive diplomacy has two parts: credible deterrence and projected deterrence. Coercive diplomacy is a good example of indirect warfare, that is, without involving the use of armed forces. In fact, optimum utilisation of media, social media, electronics, industries, diplomatic fora should be resorted to, to conduct coercive diplomacy. Look at Tibet and Kashmir, they were all exercises in coercive diplomacy. In all the examples of US conduct of coercive diplomacy, it can be seen that it is dangerous to use military directly but advantageous to resort to coercive diplomacy. Diplomacy is the furtherance of the core national interests of a country. In fact, we have adequate examples of US, China and Pakistan conducting coercive diplomacy against us. We need to drop this 'holier than thou' attitude of ours and stop being cautious and reactive and apply the same type of diplomatic tools as that of our adversaries. We also need to grow this art of coercive diplomacy. For instance, the Doklam crisis displayed a matured stance backed by the Indian Army. We need to have some kind of a rulebook—of principles and accepted norms.

Question 2. Post Uri attacks, there was a lot of talk and rhetoric, especially in the media about 'isolating' Pakistan. Do you think, in today's scenario, that a state can isolate another state? What is the meaning of isolation in the international context?
Answer 2. Isolation of Pakistan is not possible and again it's a matter of perception whether a state has been isolated or not. The Americans have taken some steps against Pakistan but it's a long way for anything fruitful to occur as it's a continuous game.

Question 3. Do you think that Track II diplomacy works? Should it be used in conjunction with coercion or as a stand-alone part?
Answer 3. No tool should be left out. Any conduit, that is, trade, social, economic or cultural must be utilised to the fullest to create leverages at all levels. Diplomacy is the shaping of international opinion. It is both the process and the target. The cost of efforts should match the

strategic environment. The end result of diplomacy is that people should be willing to fight alongside us. We should have the capability to foresee conflictual situations.

Question 4. Do you think that measures such as surgical strikes, threatening to revoke the MFN status or the IWT) have had any compellent effect against Pakistan, to stop its cross-border infiltration and terrorism against India? Is there a need to look at incipient steps in a process or does the end state only matter?

Answer 4. Surgical strikes had an advantage that we took a decision and we had the courage to openly say it out on the public forum that we had taken a decision to act. It amounted to shaping up of the cognitive domain. We must presume that it made a difference. Warfare is not a zero-sum game, it's the creation of conditions that the enemy does not interfere in. Our main fault was that we never looked at strategic solutions. It is only now that we have started opening the box of higher end strategic and military options. If nothing, we have gained the ability to create nuisance for the enemy.

Question 5. What, according to you, are the coercive measures or steps that need to be taken in order to pressurise Pakistan to accede to our demand of stopping cross border infiltration?

Answer 5. We need to develop the art of calibrating violence in Jammu and Kashmir (J&K) and also to instigate violence at our own will. We need to remember that the centre of gravity is the Pakistani army and we need to create compulsions for them. The population of the valley needs to brought to the level that they say 'Enough is Enough'. Education opportunities must be given priority. After all, governance is not nothing. If you look at the news, funds for the separatists have been cut off, one of the ground steps that have been taken. The political leadership in the Valley needs to wake up and get their act together. As a nation, we have never looked at the solution and have always managed the situation. We have been OK with the status quo. As far as engaging with Pakistan is concerned, I personally feel very low. As an Indian, it really is a low point engaging with the Pakistanis. We need to raise the level of our self-worth and benchmark ourselves with the US or at least China. We have lowered our own standards by referring to Pakistan so many times on the international forum. The quantum of importance that we accord Pakistan is not good. The day we stop being sensitive to Pakistan, China will understand that there is no point raising issues with Pakistan against us. We need to strengthen and learn the art of managing and creating sub-conventional conflicts against Pakistan. It will do wonders and increase our credibility and create in their minds a sense of our irrationality, leading to more dividends.

Appendix 'D'

Interview with Lt Gen Balraj Singh Nagal (Retd), PVSM, AVSM, SM, Former Commander in Chief Strategic Forces Command and Former Director, Centre for Land Warfare Studies (CLAWS)

Question 1. In terms of intermediate level attacks such as Pathankot and Uri, the Government of India has taken ad-hoc steps to respond. These attacks are neither too small such as arms snatching, or killing of a few civilians to elicit more than a tactical response from the local security agencies, nor large enough 'defining' events such as Mumbai or the Parliament attacks for an Operation Parakram-like response. Attacks such as these fall in the middle of the spectrum but are significant in their own sense. Pathankot, as it came in the wake of similar attacks in Pakistan such as the Mehran Air Base or the Karachi Naval Base where two refurbished and state-of-the-art P3C Orions were destroyed and Uri, which occurred just 2 months after the Burhan Wani killings came in the wake of intense nationalist outcry on the social media and the fact that 19 Indian soldiers were killed, most of them being burnt to death than by enemy fire. Various options were considered by the Indian government such as reviewing the IWT, the MFN status of Pakistan, conduct of surgical strikes, which were conspicuously absent in the aftermath of the Pathankot attacks. Do you think there is need for a rulebook, in terms of a defined National Security Policy to deal with such kind of events, where out of a host of options available to the Government, a number of permutations and combinations may be worked out to chalk out an adequate response to coerce Pakistan?

Answer 1. There should be a broad policy objective of dealing with situations like these. There is no requirement of going into specific response mechanisms. A definite National Security Policy should be instituted but not as a step-by-step response but more as a policy guideline. There should be adequate flexibility within those guidelines to allow the government to use a variety of diplomatic and coercive measures.

Question 2. Post Uri attacks, there was a lot of talk and rhetoric, especially in the media about 'isolating' Pakistan. Do you think, in today's scenario, that a state can isolate another state? What is the meaning of isolation in the international context?

Answer 2. Isolation may be possible against countries but definitely not between India and Pakistan. Pakistan has got strategic friends who will defend its position as long as they feel Pakistan fulfils their strategic objectives. There is a need to build opinions, build up a case against a country in order to start isolating it. The country needs to be shunned at important fora. The case of nonattendance by member countries to a SAARC summit to be held in Pakistan hardly merits any importance as SAARC itself is dysfunctional. Isolation is not easy. It basically implies that the country has no strategic importance or interests. In the current scenario, isolation of Pakistan especially by India is not feasible. We also have not acted maturely. There is always inadequate intelligence and we are more than ready to divulge our sources. We have been too dependent on the testimony of David Headley. If you remember, we also gave away our source on the Kargil intercepts by showing the world and especially Pakistan the conversations. It enables Pakistan to plug in their information gaps and be more secretive. To be sure, we will have to work harder to extract additional information now. Big talk and rhetoric are not good, it constricts the space for backroom diplomacy. According to me, coercive diplomacy is not always visible.

Question 3. Do you think that Track II diplomacy works? Should it be used in conjunction with coercion or as a stand-alone part?

Answer 3. Track II diplomacy is required provided the right people are chosen to conduct the same. If you have people who are in the panel or commission just for 'photo ops' or to further their own self-interests, Track II will never work. Also, this kind of interaction cannot be open-ended and has to have some kind of timeline. Track II diplomacy should also be subject-specific and limited in scope and charter and only subject experts with credibility should be made part of these delegations.

Question 4. Do you think that measures such as surgical strikes, threatening to revoke the MFN status or the IWT have had any compellent effect against Pakistan, to stop its cross-border infiltration and terrorism against India? Is there a need to look at incipient steps in a process or does the end state only matter?

Answer 4. As far as MFN status is concerned, Pakistan is not dependent on us for any major trade so revocation of MFN status will hardly make a dent in Pakistan's fortunes. The only step that seems feasible and is likely to have any effect in the future is the implied or actual threat of revocation of the IWT. Even if we withdraw from the treaty completely, we will not be able to choke Pakistan completely. However the statement or threat of withdrawal, the 'blood and water cannot flow together' speech acts as both a deterrent and a compellent measure. In spite of the 'nuclear overhang', compellence can and does work. Escalation control is comparatively easier in diplomacy as you can pull back instead of staring across the gun barrels of each other. Targeting Pakistan diplomatically and simultaneously addressing the international community requires both assertiveness and finesse. The message must go through that this kind of behaviour is not acceptable. The Prime Minister, Mr Modi, asked his secretaries to look at the mechanics and implications of withdrawing from IWT and I think the issue was well-addressed. We should not always focus on the end results. Intermediate and penultimate results must also be looked at positively, when looking at the success of compellence measures. Look at the case of North Korea, indirectly China has been coerced to rein in the Kim Jong-un regime. A mature policy that evolves over a period of time and leaves space for flexibility is the right response to provocations like Uri. If we want to look at positive incremental steps, you must remember that Pakistan's strategy is to bleed India by a thousand cuts.

Question 5. What, according to you, are the coercive measures or steps that need to be taken in order to pressurise Pakistan to accede to our demand of stopping cross border infiltration?

Answer 5. A change in their strategy, that is, the move towards reduction or complete stoppage of cross-border terrorism is the change that we must be looking for, as vindication of our coercion measures. The political leadership of Pakistan has yet to be addressed and through these measures, we have addressed the military leadership and if the present trend of posturing continues, I think it's a step in the positive direction.

Appendix 'E'

Interview with Mr TCA Rangachari, IFS, Former Ambassador to Germany, France and Algeria, Former Director of Academy of International Studies and Distinguished Fellow, Vivekananda International Foundation (VIF)

Question 1. In terms of intermediate-level attacks such as Pathankot and Uri, the Government of India has taken ad hoc steps to respond. These attacks are neither too small such as arms snatching, or killing of a few civilians to elicit more than a tactical response from the local security agencies, nor large enough 'defining' events such as Mumbai or the Parliament attacks for an Operation Parakram-like response. Attacks such as these fall in the middle of the spectrum but are significant in their own sense. Pathankot, as it came in the wake of similar attacks in Pakistan such as the Mehran Air Base or the Karachi Naval Base where two refurbished and state-of-the-art P3C Orions were destroyed and Uri, which occurred just 2 months after the Burhan Wani killings came in the wake of intense nationalist outcry on the social media and the fact that 19 Indian soldiers were killed, most of them being burnt to death than by enemy fire. Various options were considered by the Indian government such as reviewing the IWT, the MFN status of Pakistan, conduct of surgical strikes, which were conspicuously absent in the aftermath of the Pathankot attacks. Do you think there is need for a rulebook, maybe in terms of a defined National Security Policy to deal with such kind of events, where out of a host of options available to the Government, a number of permutations and combinations may be worked out to chalk out an adequate response to coerce Pakistan?

Answer 1. Let's start with a few concepts. Who were the individuals that carried out the Uri attacks? These were individuals that came from across and were not Indian nationals. We were able to trace them to pro-Pakistan organisations. Now one option is to kill them all. Another is to assess the damage and then find ways to respond. The third option is not to do anything and be content with the fact that the attacks failed.

These are all military responses. The next question is how do I balance? Equivalence in this case is not suggested. It is difficult to determine quantum of punishment in terms of human lives. When talking about coercive diplomacy, it is also important to talk about competence and the capability to exercise coercive diplomacy. Look at the Raymond Davis affair, for example, he was a contractor who killed Pakistanis in broad daylight in Pakistan but was able to get away with it due to the inherent protection afforded to him by the coercive power of the US. Coercive diplomacy also needs to ensure within itself an unsaid threat to give a fitting or befitting response to any attacks by the other adversary.

Question 2. Post Uri attacks, there was a lot of talk and rhetoric, especially in the media about 'isolating' Pakistan. Do you think, in today's scenario, that a state can isolate another state? What is the meaning of isolation in the international context?
Answer 2. Isolation of Pakistan is not possible and again it's a matter of perception whether a state has been isolated or not. The Americans have taken some steps against Pakistan but it's a long way for anything fruitful to occur as it's a continuous game.

Question 3. Do you think that Track II diplomacy works? Should it be used in conjunction with coercion or as a stand-alone part?
Answer 3. No tool should be left out. Any conduit, that is, trade, social, economic or cultural must be utilised to the fullest to create leverages at all levels. Diplomacy is the shaping of international opinion. It is both the process and the target. The cost of efforts should match the strategic environment. The end result of diplomacy is that people should be willing to fight alongside us. We should have the capability to foresee conflictual situations.

Question 4. Do you think that measures such as surgical strikes, threatening to revoke the MFN status or the IWT have had any compellent effect against Pakistan, to stop its cross-border infiltration and terrorism against India? Is there a need to look at incipient steps in a process or does the end state only matter?

Answer 4. Surgical strikes had an advantage that we took a decision and we had the courage to openly say it out on the public forum that we had taken a decision to act. It amounted to shaping up of the cognitive domain. We must presume that it made a difference. Warfare is not a zero-sum game, it's the creation of conditions that the enemy does not interfere in. Our main fault was that we never looked at strategic solutions. It is only now that we have started opening the box of higher-end strategic and military options. If nothing, we have gained the ability to create nuisance for the enemy.

Question 5. What, according to you, are the coercive measures or steps that need to be taken in order to pressurise Pakistan to accede to our demand of stopping cross-border infiltration?

Answer 5. We need to develop the art of calibrating violence in J&K and also to instigate violence at our own will. We need to remember that the centre of gravity (CoG) is the Pakistani army and we need to create compulsions for them. The population of the valley needs to brought to the level that they say 'Enough is Enough'. Education opportunities must be given priority. After all, governance is not nothing. If you look at the news, funds for the separatists have been cut off, one of the ground steps that have been taken. The political leadership in the Valley needs to wake up and get their act together. As a nation, we have never looked at the solution and have always managed the situation. We have been OK with the status quo. As far as engaging with Pakistan is concerned, I personally feel very low. As an Indian, it really is a low point engaging with the Pakistanis. We need to raise the level of our self-worth and benchmark ourselves with the US or at least China. We have lowered our own standards by referring to Pakistan so many times on the international forum. The quantum of importance that we accord Pakistan is not good. The day we stop being sensitive to Pakistan, China will understand that there is no point raising issues with Pakistan against us. We need to strengthen and learn the art of managing and creating sub-conventional conflicts against Pakistan. It will do wonders and increase our credibility and create in their minds a sense of our irrationality, leading to more dividends.

Appendix 'F'

Interview with Ms Dhanasree Jayaram, Project Associate at Manipal Advanced Research Group at Department of Geopolitics and International Relations

Question 1. Considering the varied level of attacks on the Indian state, ranging from low-level tactical attacks to intermediate-level attacks such as Uri and Pathankot and finally mega events such as Mumbai and Parliament, do you think India should have a playbook or a rulebook of sorts where it lists down the measures and actions that it can take in terms of the measures to be taken in case similar attacks happen again?
Answer. It's a matter of perception. Of course, any country with a national security strategy that lists out its priorities, capabilities and response strategies is known as a great power. In our case, since we have had a soft approach towards terrorism for long, we are indeed being taken for granted. And ad hoc responses are not in our interest in the long run. We can remain unpredictable to our enemy even when we have a rulebook—that's what Arthashastra is all about. Just that we have forgotten our ancient history.

Question 2. Is isolation of a country by another possible country in today's times? Was isolation of Pakistan fruitful or credible post Uri?
Answer. To some extent, it at least sent out a strong message and we are slowly seeing results wherein countries like the US have also started to distance from Pakistan. However, this may not be entirely feasible considering we have countries like China that will never really disengage with Pakistan. Even in the upcoming BRICS summit, China wants to ensure that Pakistan and terrorism won't be brought up by India. So, isolation is theoretically and practically not easy unless there is a global consensus on imposing sanctions and such other measures to completely isolate Pakistan. Even the efficacy of sanctions can be questioned if you look at the case of North Korea or even Iran.

Question 3. Is there a need for Track 2 diplomacy in parallel with coercion?
Answer. We must remember that the Pakistan Army and the ISI are not the same as the civilian government; and none of them probably represent the wishes of the common people on the streets. We must also understand that Pakistan is a divided country and through Track 2 diplomacy, we should try and build more and more long-term connections with Baluchistan, Sindh etc. The people of Punjab and Sindh (especially the latter) are more interested in doing business and trade with India than engage in conflict or promote cross-border terrorism. These sentiments, we must respect, and try to absorb into the dialogue.

Question 4. Do we always look at the end state or also the initiation of a process when looking at success of compellence?
Answer. I'm not an expert on this topic.

Question 5. How serious is the problem of coordinated signalling in a democracy like India as compared to that attempted by Pakistan?
Answer. This is a really broad topic and can't be answered in a few sentences. If you are asking a leading question in terms of looking at the cons of a democracy in opposition to a military-intelligence led government in Pakistan that does not need the coordination of bureaucracy and other agents of a democratic government, of course, to the outside world, it might look like India is unable to give a coordinated signalling. However, we see that this is changing. We also have had problems in terms of mobilising opinion in a state like J&K because of groups like Hurriyat that openly takes money from Pakistan ISI to spew trouble in the state. With these divisions, and the lack of political will to give free hand to the military in containing the menace (which has changed now), most of our actions remained in speeches and statements; and very less of military signalling, despite the fact that conventionally we are far superior.

Question 6. Have aggressive military strategies on both sides worsened the conflict resolution mechanism between the two countries?

Answer. From whatever has happened so far, the only thing that's derailing the peace talks or conflict resolution mechanisms is cross-border terrorism. And now you have the added problem of China occupying our territory as well. It's the covert and overt military strategy of Pakistan that has indeed created fissures.

Question 7. Finally, have steps such as surgical strikes, review of Indus Water Treaty, review of MFN status really portrayed India's position as a state willing to utilise coercive diplomacy as a tool of statecraft against Pakistan?

Answer. On Indus, India has now mellowed down after the initial rhetoric of 'water and blood cannot flow together' by Modi. In fact, India is now sitting down with Pakistan in New York, discussing how to go about the dispute resolution process. Surgical strikes were a one-off thing that we should have done after the Mumbai attacks itself, but we didn't. This is surely a beginning in terms of using coercive diplomacy as we continue to engage with Pakistan (we can't afford to stop talking, it's our neighbour—the burden of geography). However, we have to wait and see how far the government is ready to go.

Appendix 'G'

Interview with Mr Pinaki Bhattacharya, Contributor at Vivekananda International Foundation (VIF)

Surgical Strikes

Surgical strikes naturally have high degree of value in terms of coercion. But the overall impact of that can be contained by the State of the subject country if it can control the domestic media from reporting the fallout in entirety. However, the realisation of cost of action/s by the Subject country has to be disproportionately high, yet being below the optimum threshold for pain. This fine calibration in terms of military operations is naturally more difficult than when not backed by suitable diplomatic manoeuvres.

UN Ivy League of Terror Speech

The UN is naturally a location of talking shop but it can only be substantive in terms of coercive value if there is lobbying the member-nations and being strongly backed by the Permanent Five (P-5).

Forward Deployments in Punjab, Rajasthan and J&K

This is not really a coercive measure unless it is seen as an instrument of pre-emptive measures backed by actionable intelligence.

Evacuation of Border Villages

Evacuation of border villages has a limited value unless there is a well-publicised plan to launch for cross-border ops, which can even lead to a border war.

Review of MFN Status

Very limited value unless the subject country is a substantial trade partner.

Review of Indus Water Treaty

The review is an issue that actually has wider ramifications touching the lives of the common people. This has twin effects: one, it has an immense psychological setback as a part of warfare of psychological operations. And two, it can actually cause pain to the common people thus letting them into the realm of rebelling against the ruling elite.

The subject of International Relations is really in terms of generalised theories. Its application is witnessed in the making of foreign policy which can be multi-disciplinary. Hence don't see much scope for South Asia-specific IR theory, unless you believe in Chanakyan prescription, which is again limited in scope in terms of philosophical thought. Quantification of policy instruments as a measure can be effective if the coordinates can be correctly valued. You cannot have an SOP with sufficient flexibility for limited improvisation that I assume you are seeking (reference your second para) unless you have the declaratory codes of engagement like a National Security Policy etc.

Appendix 'H'

Interview with Mr Ramananda Sengupta, Foreign Affairs Editor at The New Indian Express

Surgical Strikes

If the idea behind it is to raise the costs for the Pakistani side, then these strikes need to be weighed against the possibility of escalation.

I would differentiate between surgical strikes being announced publicly and those done quietly and in secrecy. (Not retaliating for any atrocity committed on Indian troops is severely damaging to the military morale, and such strikes are usually condoned with a wink and nod).

Though there might be political compulsions behind it, the former is actually counterproductive, because it raises public expectations that such strikes will be used each time there is a terrorist attack. It does, however, ensure that Pakistan's border security goes on high alert each time there is a terror strike in India, which is both costly and stressful. Announcing a strike after it has been conducted, however, does send out a message to not just Pakistan, but also the international community that we will not sit back and keep getting hit.

UN Ivy League of Terror Speech

Again, useful, but limited impact, given that the world already knows the extent of Pakistani perfidy, but still prefers to do business with it for geostrategic and other reasons. But combined with the publicly announced surgical strike, it publicly announces India's ability and intent to hit back.

Forward Deployments in Punjab, Rajasthan and J&K

Forward deployment is useful only if we back up our ability with intent. The mobilisation and subsequent stand-down in late 2001 only reinforced the international (and Pakistani) belief that when push comes to shove, India always blinks first.

Evacuation of Border Villages

This usually happens only to protect our border population from cross-border shelling, or as a decoy move to make Pakistan believe that we might be planning something from that area.

Review of MFN Status

Given the trade volumes, a review is mostly symbolic.

Review of Indus Water Treaty

This is the most effective, and the most difficult coercive step. Pakistan has long believed that Indian control of the headwaters of the rivers that are its lifelines give it a strategic chokehold. In fact, the reason behind Pakistan's obsession with Kashmir is as much to do with capturing these headwaters as it is religious. However, river waters cannot be turned off like tap, and diversions and dams, apart from being expensive, time-consuming projects, have other compulsions, both environmental/ecological as well as strategic.

Raising the Balochistan/Baltistan Bogey

This is something that appears to have had some impact not just on Pakistan, but also its sugar daddy, China. If Balochistan remains restive, the CPEC security costs go up exponentially, ditto in Gilgit-Baltistan (GB, where there is hectic Chinese involvement in building telecommunication and other infrastructure. But while Pakistan got a taste of its own medicine, it also reduces us to their level and takes away our moral high ground (though morality has limited value in IR, particularly when it clashes with national interests)

Force comes in when diplomacy fails. But Pakistan's candid willingness to rattle its nuclear sabre the moment it perceives a threat makes a real conventional military threat somewhat iffy, which is why India refused to cross the LoC during the Kargil operations. Having said that, the policy of raising both the economic costs for Pakistani interference in India has to be supplemented by a focused outreach to undermine the army's influence in the country. Because as long as the army rules, coercive methods only help strengthen their assertion that

India is out to overrun Pakistan at the first opportunity. But given the army's increasing mingling with the civilian setup, including commerce and industry as well as service sectors like transport and food, this is again a difficult task. To revert to an old jungle saying, the only thing India can do is speak softly and carry (and sometimes use) a big stick.

Briefly, I think we are already looking at IR differently from the US idea of deterrence, simply because our challenge is somewhat different. Unlike the Americans, who revel in the big brother syndrome, our geopolitical sensitivities prevent us from using that approach, and it is only of late that we have started understanding power, to begin with. We used to be quite diffident about flaunting it earlier. However, while we are looking at new ways to resolve old problems, I don't think we have a concrete game plan yet. On the face of it, what do you do with when two immediate neighbours, both nuclear powers, gang up against you? One, without subsuming your own identity, you align with the sole superpower (still, though for how long, even God doesn't know), two, you build bridges with your other neighbours, and stress on soft power while rapidly ramping up the hard power, and three, develop—and flaunt—asymmetrical responses. Regionally, it is important to be perceived as the sober, non-hegemonistic counterpoint to an overbearing China. Modi's neighbourhood first policy seems to have hit a roadblock, but it is a step in the right direction. So are attempts to revive BIMSTEC and other similar regional groupings.

Appendix 'J'

Interview with Sarral Sharma, Researcher at Institute of Peace and Conflict Studies

Pathankot attack changed the entire policy which was further accentuated after the Burhan Wani encounter and following anti-India rhetoric by Pakistan. Afterwards, PM Modi's Independence Day speech marked the obvious change. I will discuss point by point your questions.

Coming back to your specific questions on India's coercive diplomacy towards Pakistan after the aforementioned incidents. Personally, I think the Modi government had begun its 'hard' approach toward Pakistan since August 2014 only when it cancelled the foreign secretary-level talks after the Hurriyat leaders met the Pak High Commissioner in New Delhi. Although, it was testing the waters by inviting Sharif to Modi's swearing-in ceremony. Also, the summer of 2014 in J&K was not as bloodied as it is today. Even the Pakistani establishment was looking for a window of opportunity, which was somewhat provided after dismissing separatists' role in the Kashmir issue, followed by 2014 elections in J&K and the PDP–BJP alliance in the state.

On and off bilateral engagement continued to take place like the Ufa agreement happened and we somehow managed to sideline the Kashmir issue. Pathankot attack in Jan 2016, followed by the cancellation of foreign secretary talks in Islamabad laid out the foundation of the 'coercive diplomacy'. Wani's killing was the last nail in the coffin.

Specific Incidents

Surgical Strikes

Time-bound reciprocal aggressive military posturing, followed by proactive naming and shaming Pakistan internationally for its role in fomenting terrorism in J&K. Sent jitters down the international community's spine whether India had crossed the nuclear threshold or not with the surgical strikes? Was India planning to use the 'cold start doctrine' to inflict short-term damage to Pakistan but below the nuke threshold? Nothing of that sort happened (unfortunately!). It had a high symbolic value.

UN Ivy League of Terror Speech
Tit-for-tat aggressive diplomatic response at the UN. Much needed in order to divert the international attention from the then ongoing violence in Kashmir. Presenting the other side of the conflict i.e. Pakistan's own human rights record and the 'good vs. bad Taliban' dichotomy.

Forward Deployments in Punjab, Rajasthan and J&K
Military posturing to put pressure on Pakistan; not really sure about its significance. Could have been done to create confusion for the adversary.

Evacuation of Border Villages
Precautionary measures. Pakistan too could inflict damage on the Indian side; signalled the gravity of the situation on the borders. Bit apprehensive of considering it as a part of the coercive diplomacy. May be to create panic in Pakistan of India's attention, especially after the 'surgical strikes'.

Review of MFN Status
Politically symbolic; nothing much happened though.

Review of IWT
Definitely part of the coercive diplomacy. But very limited in nature as an international organisation i.e. the World Bank is a signatory. Unsurprisingly, Pakistan played out the 'human rights' card to counter India's use of the treaty as a part of its coercive diplomacy. With China's unprecedented involvement in Pakistan, India may not be able to use it for long.

Must say one thing, most of the IR theories have failed to understand or correctly evaluate the India–Pakistan conflict, especially the Kashmir issue. Definitely, we need a separate IR framework to understand complicated nuances of the situation. Coercive diplomacy is an important tool to call Pakistan's bluff and also to inflict tactical damages. However, I still believe that India has not yet been able to find a balanced combination of the two: military and diplomacy to counter its adversaries, especially Pakistan. Yet, it's an important test case considering the Modi government is trying something new (partially) through its Pakistan policy. It turned out to be a mixed bag for us. Sidelining Pakistan at SAARC could be a tactical diplomatic win, but, we must not forget China and Russia's refusal to mention Pakistan's role in fomenting terrorism in the region at the BRICS summit. Also, smaller countries in the region such as Nepal, Maldives, to an extent Sri Lanka are not really happy with India being the 'big brother'. The recent standoff in Doklam plateau has also put some questions marks on India's relations with Bhutan, which is getting wary of the Chinese dominance in the region.

Bibliography

Primary Sources

1. Interview with Major General Pramod Kumar Saigal (Retired), Defence Expert.
2. Interview with Lieutenant General Balraj Singh Nagal, PVSM, AVSM, SM (Retired), Director, Centre for Land Warfare Studies (CLAWS).
3. Interview with Lieutenant General Philip Campose, PVSM, AVSM (Retired), Distinguished Senior Fellow, Centre for Land Warfare Studies (CLAWS).
4. Interview with Lieutenant General Gurmit Singh, PVSM, UYSM, AVSM, VSM (Retired), Distinguished Senior Fellow, Centre for Land Warfare Studies (CLAWS).
5. Interview with Mr TCA Rangachari, IFS, Former Ambassador to France, Algeria and Germany.
6. Interview with Dhanasree Jayaram, Project Associate at Manipal Advanced Study Group at Department of Geopolitics and International Relations.
7. Interview with Pinaki Bhattacharya, Contributor at Vivekananda International Foundation.
8. Interview with Ramananda Sengupta, Foreign Affairs Editor at The New Indian Express
9. Interview with Sarral Sharma, Researcher at Institute of Peace and Conflict Studies.

Secondary Sources

Books

1. P. R. Chari, Pervaiz Iqbal Cheema and Stephen P. Cohen, *Four Crises and a Peace Process* (New York, NY: Brookings Institution Press, 2009).
2. V. K. Sood and Pravin Sawhney, *Operation Parakram* (New Delhi: Sage Publications, 2006).
3. George Perkovich and Toby Dalton, *Not War Not Peace: Motivating Pakistan to Prevent Cross Border Terrorism,* 1st ed. (Oxford University Press, 2016).
4. Thomas Schelling, *Arms and Influence,* 1st ed. (Yale University Press, 1966).
5. Sumit Ganguly and Devin Hagerty, *Fearful Symmetry: India-Pakistan Crises in the Nuclear Shadow,* 1st ed. (Washington DC: University of Washington Press, 2006).
6. Alexander L. George and William Simons, *Limits of Coercive Diplomacy,* 2nd ed. (Michigan: Westview Press, 1994).
7. Wallace J. Thies, *When Governments Collide* (Berkeley: University of California Press, 1980).
8. Lawrence Freedman, *Deterrence* (Polity, 2004).
9. Bernard Brodie and Frederick Dunn, *The absolute weapon* (Freeport, N.Y.: Books for Libraries Press, 1972).
10. Arnold Wolfers, *Discord and Collaboration: Essays on International Politics* (Michigan: Johns Hopkins University Press, 1965).

11. Eric Herring, *Danger and Opportunity: Explaining International Crisis Outcomes,* 1st ed. (Manchester: Manchester University Press, 1995).
12. Khaled Ahmed,*Sleepwalking to Surrender* (n.d.).
13. Christine Fair, *Fighting to the End: The Pakistan Army's Way of War,* 1st ed. (Oxford: Oxford University Press, 2014).
14. Myra MacDonald, *Defeat is an Orphan,* 1st ed. (Penguin Random House India, 2017).
15. V. P. Malik, *Kargil: From Surprise To Victory,* 2nd ed. (Harper Collins, 2011).
16. Mark Tully and Satish Jacob, *Amritsar: Mrs Gandhi's Last Battle,* 2nd ed. (New Delhi: Rupa Publications, 2010).
17. Husain Haqqani, *Magnificent Delusions,* 3rd ed. ([Place of publication not identified]: Perseus Books Group, 2013).
18. Krishnaswamy Sundarji, *Blind Men of Hindoostan,* 1st ed. (New Delhi: Soma Books Ltd, 1994).
19. Adrian Levy and Cathy Scott-Clark, *The Siege: The Attack on the Taj,* 1st ed. (Penguin Books Limited, 2015).
20. Anatol Lieven, *Pakistan: A Hard Country* (Penguin, 2011).
21. Stanley Wolpert, *Jinnah of Pakistan* (Oxford: Oxford University Press, 2005).
22. Husain Haqqani, *Pakistan: Between Mosque and Military,* 1st ed. (Viking, 2016).
23. Ayesha Jalal, *The Sole Spokesman: Jinnah, the Muslim League and the Demand for Pakistan* (Cambridge: Cambridge University Press, 1985).
24. Stephen P. Cohen, *The Idea of Pakistan* (Oxford: Oxford University Press, 2006).
25. Husain Haqqani, *Reimagining Pakistan: Transforming a Dysfunctional Nuclear State,* 1st ed. (New Delhi: Harper Collins India, 2018).
26. Kim Barker, *The Taliban Shuffle: Strange Days in Afghanistan and Pakistan,* 2nd ed. (Anchor, 2012).
27. Carlotta Gall, *The Wrong Enemy* (New Delhi: Penguin Books India, 2015).
28. Steve Coll, *Ghost Wars: The Secret History of the CIA, Afghanistan and Bin Laden, from the Soviet Invasion to September* 10, 2001, 1st ed. (London: Penguin UK, 2005).
29. Ijaz Khan, *Pakistan's Strategic Culture & Foreign Policy Making: A Study of Pakistan's Post 9/11 Afghan Policy Change (Politics and Economics of the Middle East),* 1st ed. (Nova Science Publishers Inc, 2018).
30. Tilak Devasher, *Pakistan: Courting the Abyss,* 1st ed. (Harpercollins, 2016).
31. Gary Clyde Hufbauer et al., *Economic Sanctions Reconsidered,* 3rd ed. (Peterson Institute for International Economics, 2009).

Journals

32. Benjamin S. Lambeth, "Airpower at 18,000': The Indian Air Force in the Kargil War," [online] *Carnegie Endowment for International Peace.* https://carnegieendowment.org/2012/09/20/airpower-at-18-000-indian-air-force-in-kargil-war-event-3777, accessed on September 11, 2017.
33. Angel Rabasa et al., *The Lessons of Mumbai* (Online Research Library: Questia, 2004). [online] https://www.questia.com/library/120080764/the-lessons-of-mumbai, accessed on May 05, 2017.
34. Maria Sperandei, "Bridging Deterrence and Compellence: An Alternative Approach to the Study of Coercive Diplommacy," *International Studies Review* [online] vol. 8, no. 2, 2006, pp. 253–280. https://onlinelibrary.wiley.com/doi/abs/10.1111/j.1468-2486.2006.00573.x

35. Karl Mueller, "Strategies of Coercion: Denial, Punishment, and the Future of Air Power,"*Security Studies*, [online] vol. 7, no. 3, 1998, pp.182–228. https://www.tandfonline.com/doi/abs/10.1080/09636419808429354
36. David Carter, "The Compellence Dilemma: International Disputes with Violent Groups," *International Studies Quarterly*, [online] vol. 59, no. 3, 2015, pp.461–476. https://onlinelibrary.wiley.com/doi/abs/10.1111/isqu.12192
37. Patrick C. Bratton, "When is Coercion Successful?," *Naval War College Review*, [online] vol. 58, no. 3, 2005. http://digital-commons.usnwc.edu/nwc-review/vol58/iss3/6/
38. Paul Gordon Lauren, "Ultimata and Coercive Diplomacy," *International Studies Quarterly*, vol. 16, no. 2, 1972, pp. 131–166. https://doi.org/10.2307/3013977
39. Walter J. Petersen, "Deterrence and Compellence: A Critical Assessment of Conventional Wisdom,"*International Studies Quarterly*, [online] vol. 30, no. 3, 1986, pp. 269–294. http://www.jstor.org/stable/2600418.
40. Glenn H. Snyder, "Deterrence and Power," *The Journal of Conflict Resolution*, [online] vol. 4, no. 2, 1960, pp. 163–178. http://www.jstor.org/stable/172650
41. David A. Baldwin, "Power Analysis and World Politics: New Trends versus Old Tendencies," *World Politics*, [online] vol. 31, no. 2, 1979, pp. 161–194. http://www.jstor.org/stable/2009941
42. Robert J. Art and Patrick M. Cronin, "The United States and Coercive Diplomacy,"*Political Science Quarterly*, [online] vol. 119, no. 3, 2013, pp. 536–537. https://doi.org/10.2307/20202404
43. Mea.gov.in., "Indus Waters Treaty," [online] (1960). http://mea.gov.in/bilateral-documents.htm?dtl/6439/Indus
44. Shakil Ahmad Romshoo, "Assessing the Influence of Watershed Characteristics on the Flood Vulnerability of Jhelum Basin in Kashmir Himalaya," *Natural Hazards*, [online] https://www.researchgate.net/publication/277832264_Assessing_the_influence_of_watershed_characteristics_on_the_flood_vulnerability_of_Jhelum_Basin_in_Kashmir_Himalaya_reply_to_comment_by Shah_2015
45. Walter C. Ladwig III, "A Cold Start for Hot Wars? The Indian Army's New Limited War Doctrine," *International Security* vol. 32, no. 3, 2007, pp.158–190.
46. Peter Viggo Jakobsen, "Western Use of Coercive Diplomacy after the Cold War: A Challenge for Theory and Practice," *International Journal* vol. 54, no. 4, 1999, pp. 509–510.
47. Jack Levy, "Deterrence and Coercive Diplomacy: The Contributions of Alexander George," *Political Psychology* vol. 29, no. 4, 2008, pp. 537–552.
48. Asif Siddiqui, "From Deterrence and Coercive Diplomacy to War: The 1971 Crisis in South Asia," *Journal of International and Area Studies* vol. 4, no. 1, 1997, pp. 73–92.
49. Fiona McGillivray and Allan Stam, "Political Institutions, Coercive Diplomacy, and the Duration of Economic Sanctions," *Journal of Conflict Resolution* vol. 48, no. 2, 2004, pp.154–172.
50. Bruce W. Jentleson, "The Reagan Administration and Coercive Diplomacy: Restraining More Than Remaking Governments," *Political Science Quarterly* vol. 106, no. 1, 1991, p. 57.
51. Gregory F. Treverton and Alexander L. George, "Forceful Persuasion: Coercive Diplomacy as an Alternative to War," *Foreign Affairs* vol. 71, no. 3, 1992, p. 169.
52. Janice Stein, "Crisis Management: Looking Back to Look Forward," *Political Psychology* vol. 29, no. 4, 2008, pp. 553–569.

53. Kyle Haynes, "Lame Ducks and Coercive Diplomacy," *Journal of Conflict Resolution* vol. 56, no. 5, 2012, pp. 771–798.
54. Peter Viggo Jakobsen, "Pushing the Limits of Military Coercion Theory," *International Studies Perspectives*, vol. 12, no. 2, 2011, pp. 153–170.
55. Robert Mandel, "The Effectiveness of Gunboat Diplomacy," *International Studies Quarterly* vol. 30, no. 1, 1986, p. 59.
56. Charles Kirchofer, "Targeted Killings and Compellence: Lessons from the Campaign against Hamas in the Second Intifada," *Perspectives on Terrorism* vol. 10, no. 3, 2016, pp. 16–25.
57. Janice Stein, "Deterrence and Compellence in the Gulf, 1990-91: A Failed or Impossible Task?," *International Security* vol. 17, no. 2, 1992, p. 147.
58. Walter Petersen, "Deterrence and Compellence: A Critical Assessment of Conventional Wisdom," *International Studies Quarterly* vol. 30, no. 3, 1986, p. 269.
59. Todd Sechser and Matthew Fuhrmann, "Crisis Bargaining and Nuclear Blackmail," *International Organization* vol. 67, no. 01, 2013, pp. 173–195.

Newspaper Reports

60. Syed Hasnain, "Nagrota in Perspective: It is Just One of the Thousand Cuts by Which Pakistan Hopes to Bleed India," [online] *Times of India Blog,* (2018). https://blogs.timesofindia.indiatimes.com/toi-edit-page/nagrota-in-perspective-it-is-just-one-of-the-thousand-cuts-by-which-pakistan-hopes-to-bleed-india/, accessed on July 05, 2017.
61. Jonathan Beale, "BBC NEWS|World|South Asia|US 'threatened to bomb' Pakistan," [online] *News.bbc.co.uk,* (2018). http://news.bbc.co.uk/2/hi/south_asia/5369198.stm, accessed on June 12, 2018.
62. https://www.livemint.com/, "Understanding Pakistan's New Terror Strategy," [online] (2017). https://www.livemint.com/Opinion/u8qPE1aAPuUG8SXo19SsEO/Understanding-Pakistans-new-terror-strategy.html, accessed on June 12, 2017.
63. Richa Taneja, "Parliament Attack Anniversary: Here's What Happened On December 13, 2001, And After," [online] *NDTV.com,* (2011). https://www.ndtv.com/india-news/parliament-attack-anniversary-heres-what-happened-on-december-13-2001-and-after-1787198, accessed on October 07, 2017.
64. Firstpost, A Year on from Uri Attack: Surgical Strikes, Elimination of Terrorists and Everything Else that Happened after Audacious Raid," [online] *Firstpost,* (2017). https://www.firstpost.com/india/a-year-on-from-uri-attack-surgical-strikes-elimination-of-terrorists-and-everything-else-that-happened-after-audacious-raid-4054609.html, accessed on January 18, 2018.
65. Maninder Dabas, "Here are Major Long Term War Doctrines Adopted by India and Pakistan over the Years," *Idiatimes,* https://www.indiatimes.com/news/india/with-tensions-soaring-high-once-again-here-are-major-war-doctrines-exercised-by-india-pakistan-over-the-years-262273.html, accessed on June 12, 2017.
66. "All You Need to know about the 7/11 Mumbai Train Blasts," [online] *The Hindu,* (2018). http://www.thehindu.com/news/cities/mumbai/all-you-need-to-know-about-711/article7640887.ece, accessed on October 25, 2017.
67. Pranab Dhal Samanta, "11/26/2008: How India Debated a War With Pakistan that November," [online] *Pakistanis for Peace,* (2010). http://archive.indianexpress.com/news/2611-how-india-debated-a-war-with-pakistan-that-november/716240/, accessed on December 20, 2017.
68. https://www.livemint.com/, "Understanding Pakistan's New Terror Strategy," [online]

Livemint, (2016).https://www.livemint.com/Opinion/u8qPE1aAPuUG8SXo19SsEO/Understanding-Pakistans-new-terror-strategy.html, accessed on August 12, 2017.

69. dawn.com, "Pakistan to get Leftover Afghan War Equipment: Defence Secretary," [online] *Dawn,* (2014). https://www.dawn.com/news/1096837, accessed on November 19, 2017.
70. The Hindu, "Text of Sushma Swaraj's speech at U.N. General Assembly," [online] *The Hindu,* (2017).http://www.thehindu.com/news/resources/text-of-sushma-swaraj-speech-at-un-general-assembly/article19746157.ece
71. Nikhila Nataranjan, "Who Coined 'Ivy League of Terrorism' and how India found Language of Rebuttal against Pak," [online] *Firstpost,* (2016). https://www.firstpost.com/world/who-wrote-ivy-league-of-terrorism-rebuttal-against-pak-3016626.html
72. US Congressman Ted Poe, "Chairman Poe Introduces the Pakistan State Sponsor of Terrorism Designation Act," [online] (2016). https://poe.house.gov/2016/9/chairman-poe-introduces-the-pakistan-state-sponsor-of-terrorism-designation-act
73. A. B. Wire, Put Pressure on US Government to End Pakistani Terror Strategy: Taranjit Sandhu tells Indian Americans," [online] *The American Bazaar,* (2018). https://www.americanbazaaronline.com/2016/10/10/put-pressure-on-us-government-to-end-pakistani-terror-strategy-taranjit-sandhu-tells-indian-americans-418095/, accessed on October 15, 2017.
74. Bharti Jain, "Baloch Leader Brahamdagh Bugti's Plea for Asylum on Hold?," [online] *The Times of India,* (2017). https://timesofindia.indiatimes.com/india/bugtis-plea-for-asylum-on-hold/articleshow/56725500.cms
75. Rahul Singh, "Uri Attack: Army Talks Tough, says India Reserves Right to Retaliate," [online] *Hindustan Times,* (2016). https://www.hindustantimes.com/india-news/uri-attack-army-says-india-reserves-right-to-retaliate/story-5iyNlZVceIMxuWMA5I1LcN.html
76. Fab-aviation-group.proboards.com, "Indian Deal for 36 Rafales Moves Forward," [online] *FAB—Aviation Group,* (2016). http://fab-aviation-group.proboards.com/thread/4039/
77. Jayanth Jacob, "Blood and Water can't flow together, says Modi at meeting on Indus treaty," [online] *Hindustan Times,* (2016). https://www.hindustantimes.com/india-news/blood-and-water-can-t-flow-together-says-modi-at-meeting-on-indus-treaty/story-qgZw1iAsxMli7q7hTKj4DL.html
78. The Hindu, "SAARC summit to be cancelled," [online] *The Hindu,* (2016). http://www.thehindu.com/news/international/SAARC-summit-to-be-cancelled/article15004093.ece, [Accessed 2017].
79. Nitin A. Gokhale, "The Inside Story of India's 2016 'Surgical Strikes'," [online] *The Diplomat,* (2017). https://thediplomat.com/2017/09/the-inside-story-of-indias-2016-surgical-strikes/, accessed on November 18, 2017.
80. Catherine Shoard, "Indian Film Producers Ban Pakistani Actors 'for ever' over Kashmir Crisis," [online] *The Guardian,* (2016). https://www.theguardian.com/film/2016/sep/30/indian-film-producers-motion-pictures-association-imppa-ban-pakistani-actors-crew-kashmir-crisis-escalates, accessed on October 21, 2017.
81. The Hindu, "India to Review MFN Status to Pakistan on Thursday," [online] *The Hindu,* (2016).: http://www.thehindu.com/news/national/India-to-review-MFN-status-to-Pakistan-on-Thursday/article15002296.ece, accessed September 05, 2017.
82. Franz-Stefan Gady, "India's Air Force Interested in 36 More Rafale Fighter Jets From France," [online] *The Diplomat*, (2017). https://thediplomat.com/2017/08/indias-air-

force-interested-in-36-more-rafale-fighter-jets-from-france/,accessed on December 2017.

83. Brahma Chellaney, "Water Shortages could Trigger Asia Conflicts," [online] *Stagecraft and Statecraft,* (2017). https://chellaney.net/2017/12/31/water-shortages-could-trigger-asia-conflicts/, accessed on December 06, 2017.
84. Amitabh Sinha, "Turning off Indus Tap Easier Said than Done," [online] *The Indian Express,* (2016). http://indianexpress.com/article/explained/india-pakistan-relation-indus-water-treaty-terrorism-3044967/, accessed on October 20, 2017.
85. Rosencranz, A. and Joseph, M, "By Building the Sawalkot Dam, is India Using Water as a Weapon against Pakistan?," [online] *The Wire,* (2017). https://thewire.in/external-affairs/sawalkot-dam-india-pakistan, accessed on October 2017.
86. Sameer Yasir, "Indus Waters Treaty, the Tulbul Project and its Implications on India-Pakistan relations—Firstpost," [online] *Firstpost,* (2016). https://www.firstpost.com/india/indus-waters-treaty-the-tulbul-project-and-its-implications-on-india-pakistan-relations-3022076.html, accessed on July 19, 2017.
87. Suhasini Haider, "Mission 'SAARC minus Pakistan'," [online] *The Hindu,* (2016). http://www.thehindu.com/news/national/Mission-%E2%80%98SAARC-minus-Pakistan%E2%80%99/article15005693.ece, accessed on September 23, 2017.
88. Wto.org, "WTO|Understanding the WTO—What is the World Trade Organization?," [online] *World Trade Organization,* (n.d.). https://www.wto.org/english/thewto_e/whatis_e/tif_e/fact1_e.htm, accessed on June 15, 2017.
89. Shailja Singh, "Protecting India's trade interests, [online] *The Hindu,* (2016). http://www.thehindu.com/opinion/columns/world-view-column-protecting-indias-trade-interests/article8194376.ece, accessed on November 14, 2017.
90. Tradingeconomics.com, "Pakistan Foreign Direct Investment|2010–2018|Data|Chart|Calendar," [online] *Trading Economics,* (2018). https://tradingeconomics.com/pakistan/foreign-direct-investment, accessed on January 02, 2018.
91. Press Trust of India, "China Extends Technical Hold on Masood Azhar's Terror Listing at the UN," [online] *Hindustan Times,* (2017). https://www.hindustantimes.com/world-news/china-extends-technical-hold-on-jem-chief-masood-azhar-at-the-un/story-2UWhREGfhF11gULeXIjuRK.html, accessed on September 16, 2017.